OBTAINABLE

CHRIS SARNO

Obtainable:
Revealing the Process of Faith
To Receive the Promises of God

Copyright © 2020 By Chris Sarno

Miracle House Publishing
920 Beville Rd.
Daytona Beach, FL 32114
386-257-4622

All rights reserved under International Copyright Law. Contents and/or cover may not be reproduced in whole or in part in any form without the express written consent of the Publisher.

ISBN 978-0-9815147-4-1
Library of Congress
Printed in the United States of America.

ACKNOWLEDGEMENTS

To my beautiful wife, Liz, what a journey we are on fulfilling the call that God has placed upon our lives. Thank you for your never-ending commitment to serve God and your family. Thank you for your love and support in everything I do. Your faithfulness and grace are incredible. I love you endlessly.

To my daughter Lauren, you took the message I preached and processed it into the words we read in this book. Your hard work, tireless dedication, love for God, and honor far outweigh our expectations and for that, I am grateful.

To my son Luca and my daughter Giana, my prayer for you both is that the wisdom found in this book will forever change your relationship with God, as you learn how to unlock and receive the promises He has for you.

To my family as a whole, I love you all more than you will ever know. I promise to spend the rest of my life showing you that.

TABLE OF CONTENTS

INTRODUCTION..........................i

CHAPTER ONE............................1

CHAPTER TWO.........................19

CHAPTER THREE....................37

CHAPTER FOUR.......................55

CHAPTER FIVE........................73

CHAPTER SIX...........................91

CHAPTER SEVEN....................111

ABOUT THE AUTHOR..............131

INTRODUCTION

Over the years, I've had the honor and privilege of traveling the world to share the gospel of Jesus. I've experienced incredible moves of God, witnessed countless miracles, built strong relationships that transcend culture and geography, seen incredible views, eaten delicious foods, and created memories that will last a lifetime. Interestingly enough, the most substantial takeaway that I have from walking in ministry has little to do with those things.

As a pastor, regardless of whether I'm traveling or leading my church, my job is people. And if a lifetime committed to helping people has taught me one thing, it's that deep down, we are all the same. Regardless of who you are, where you're from, how old you are, what you do for a living, etc. we all have basic desires, needs, and abilities that create our reality.

Consider this. If I were to walk up to a person on the street, in any location, and asked the question, "If you could have whatever you want, what would it be?" I can guarantee you that person would be able to give me an answer within seconds. Think about it. Whether he or she responded with a specific material object (i.e., money, clothing, housing) or something a little less tangible (i.e., happiness, health, family), everyone could answer that question with some degree of a request. Why? Because at the root, we are all the same. We might not want the same things, but we all want something.

This is a good thing. This is how God designed us. Throughout the Bible, there are countless stories of people who had a desire for something. Whether they wanted a family, a home, a purpose, health, provision, protection, insert your example here, some of the most prominent figures in the Bible are recognized because they had a desire for something, and they saw that desire fulfilled.

But it's not the fulfillment that got them their place on the pages of the Bible, but the process that it took to receive that fulfillment. Because here's the thing, God didn't fulfill those desires because those people were His favorites. They weren't fulfilled because those people had served God all of their lives. They weren't fulfilled because they were perfect, because they had all the answers, because they were wealthy, because they were famous, because they were pretty. No, not even close. Every desire and promise that God has ever fulfilled started and ended with one thing.

Faith.

That simple five-letter word can change your life. It bypasses any qualification and characteristic you could think of and helps you obtain every desire you've ever wanted in life simply based on your willingness to understand and use it correctly.

As I said, I've been blessed to visit many places and meet a lot of people. Through those experiences, I've come in contact with countless examples of people who desperately want or need something. In some instances, it's literally been life or death. The sad reality is, and please hear my heart on this; they've been praying and hoping and waiting for a promise that will likely never come to pass. Not because their desires are wrong, but because they aren't using the right tools. And that is why I've written this book. Because one of the most substantial takeaways I've had in ministry is that time, money, experience, spiritual maturity, relationship status, etc. don't change a thing, only faith can. Faith is the only qualification in the life of the believer.

I want to help you understand faith in a way, perhaps, you never have. Not in a fragmented, fragile, or theoretical state, but in its incredible entirety, so that you don't spend a lifetime waiting for something that you could have used faith to receive in an instant.

So before we get started, I want to leave you with a question. It's one that you should be familiar with because I asked it just a couple of pages ago: If you could have whatever you want, what would it be? It might be a new house, healing in your body, a promotion at work, a spouse, a child, a car, more money, less worry, peace, purpose. The list could go on. Whatever it is, as long as it aligns with the Word and will of God, I want to help you understand how to receive it.

As you read through the next pages and chapters, my goal is that you learn to utilize faith to obtain the deepest desires and needs of your heart, all while drawing closer to the One who put them there. We might not want the same things, but we all want something. I pray that you walk away from reading this book, having the answer to receiving everything you've ever wanted in life.

CHAPTER ONE
FAITH FUNDAMENTALS

We all have moments in life that we will never forget. Moments that defined us and propelled us forward. Often, when you think of those moments, you think of tangible, life-changing events like the day you got married, had a baby, got a new job, moved to a new city, or even when you got saved. There are other less tangible moments, though, that can leave just as big of an impact.

One of those less-tangible-but-life-changing moments happened to me while I was in Bible college many years ago. When I was in school, I had my own window cleaning company. I would go to my classes and special services, do my school work, and then spend any extra time cleaning the windows of local businesses. One of those local businesses was a bridal shop. I got to know the owner of the shop over time, and because she knew I was in Bible school, she would often have me pray over her business. There was one particular Friday night that I was sitting at home, not doing anything. I remember thinking, "maybe I should go pray or do something productive." But I didn't.

The next morning, as I went out on my Saturday window cleaning route, I came to the bridal shop. I saw the owner and said hello, like usual, but she wasn't herself. Something seemed off. After she attended to a customer in the store, she finally came to tell me what was wrong. She had a very aggressive form of cancer, and even though she was a believer, she was absolutely devastated. She asked if I could pray with her. As I was outside cleaning the windows, I felt awful. I remember thinking about how I could've better prepared for that moment. How I could have prayed the night before, and I didn't, or maybe how I could've been more qualified to pray for this lady at that moment. Perhaps I could have fasted or spent more time with God, and then I would have been able to have the level of faith that she needed to overcome this sickness in her body.

As I was beating myself up, God spoke to me. And this is the moment that I will remember for the rest of my life. All of a sudden, I felt God say, "By the way, when did you become the healer?" He went on to ask, "where's your faith meter at?" Instantly, I visualized a gas gauge. Looking back to my lack of preparation the night before, I started thinking, "how effective is my faith?" Do I have a full tank of faith? Half a tank? Is my tank on empty? Before I could even process my answer, God spoke again. He said, "Faith is not a container; faith is an obtainer. If you give me a keyhole's worth, I can shove a miracle through it." At that moment, my perception and understanding of faith were changed forever. All of a sudden, I felt full of faith. I went back into the bridal shop, ready to pray for the owner with no sign of intimidation or disqualification. From that moment forward, I never saw faith as a container again. I only saw faith the way that God intended it to be used: as an obtainer. It is the key to receiving every promise and blessing Heaven has to offer.

FAITH IS YOURS

Before we get any closer to understanding the ins and outs of faith, I need to clarify one crucial thing:

faith is yours. You have access to as much faith as anyone who has or will walk the face of the Earth. Romans 5:1 (MSG) tells us, "By entering through faith into what God has always wanted to do for us—set us right with him, make us fit for him—we have it all together with God because of our Master Jesus." This means that when you become a believer and accept Jesus as your Lord and Savior, you are instantly in right-standing with God; you are made righteous. Ultimately, you never have to strive to achieve any position that you have in God. We are righteous because He made us righteous when we believed in and accepted Jesus.

Before we can ever understand faith and how to operate in it, we have to have a revelation of our righteousness. We have to lose any inferiority complex that might try to disqualify us based on our past or present performance. As you learn more about faith, it's essential never to limit God's ability based on your performance. You can't look at what you have done to determine what God can do. You have to understand that you have everything you need positionally the moment you accept Jesus as your Lord and Savior.

When you walk in this level of righteousness, you can approach God without intimidation and complete boldness. The best example I can think of to illustrate this is Jesus. Throughout the gospel accounts of His life, we see the greatest miracles and operation of faith in the Bible. When Jesus came to the Earth, He was confined by the same human nature that you and I operate in. Though He was completely God, He was also completely man. This means that Jesus had no physical advantage over us (i.e., He wasn't born with indestructible superpowers like Super Man). He shared in our humanity, yet was able to manifest the most profound spiritual accomplishments that this world has ever seen.

So what was it that set Jesus apart? Obviously, He's Jesus. That's a good place to start. But if the feeble condition of man confined Jesus, there had to be something that enabled Him to produce the caliber of miracles He did while walking the face of the Earth. I believe what allowed Jesus to supersede the limitation of the Earth was His position. Though He was a man, He knew He was the Son of God. He knew His heavenly position and the authority that He possessed could bypass His humanity and allow Him to operate in His deity. Jesus approached God with a positional purity, knowing that nothing separated Him from God and God's systems, which allowed Him to operate freely in those systems.

Jesus approached God without a trace of inferiority. Because He was blameless and never sinned, He knew that there was nothing that could disqualify Him from the power of God operating in His life. Through His death on the cross, and our belief in His saving power, we are also given the same availability to approach God without a trace of inferiority. Jesus gave us His faith when He gave us the opportunity to believe in Him through His sacrifice.

As you begin to develop an understanding of faith and how it can work in your life, always remember that faith is yours. You have every right to receive what faith can bring you, and nothing you have done or will do can limit what God can do in your life.

GOD WANTS TO

There's one more thing that I'd like to address before we start talking about faith. Because I think one of the biggest problems we have when it comes to walking in faith is not failing to believe God can do anything, but failing to believe He can do anything for you. If I asked most people if they thought God could do the impossible, they would likely say yes. If I asked them if they thought God could do the impossible for them, they might not be able to answer as confidently. We know God is a healer because Isaiah 53:5 (KJV) says, "with His stripes we are healed." But when you're feeling under the weather, how much more difficult is it to believe that He truly can heal your body? Theory is always challenged in the presence of application.

This is why it is so important to understand the nature of God. James 1:5 (AMP) tells us: "If any of you lacks wisdom [to guide him through a decision or circumstance], he is to ask of [our benevolent] God, who gives to everyone generously and without rebuke or blame, and it will be given to him." In this instance, the verse refers to God giving wisdom, but the words that the Bible uses to describe Him are "benevolent" and "generous." That is the nature of our God. He doesn't hold back blessing. He wants nothing more than to give to you. He doesn't want just to do something; He wants to do something for you.

This foundational truth that God can do it for you is vital to understanding faith because it enables you to approach God with boldness. Again, Jesus is the best example of what the proper understanding of the nature of God can enable you to do. When we look to see how Jesus approached His Father, what do we see? He went to God with great confidence, He was never hesitant, and He was never shy. Jesus understood His Father's will and His Father's heart. His boldness came from His understanding of the true nature of God.

There's such a profound truth in Romans 8:31-32 (MSG) that reveals this nature even further. There it says:

> "So, what do you think? With God on our side like this, how can we lose? If God didn't hesitate to put everything on the line for us, embracing our condition and exposing himself to the worst by sending his own Son, is there anything else he wouldn't gladly and freely do for us?"

In addition to His position and authority, another thing that set Jesus apart was His awareness of the generosity and love that His Father had for Him. Imagine what you can accomplish when you understand that God cares just the same about you. Once you know the heart of God, it becomes a lot easier to operate in His systems. No matter what you're utilizing faith for, remember that God not only can do it for you, He wants to do it for you.

> NO MATTER WHAT YOU'RE UTILIZING FAITH FOR, REMEMBER THAT GOD NOT ONLY CAN DO IT FOR YOU, HE WANTS TO DO IT FOR YOU

One of the most foundational scriptures on faith is in Mark 11:24 (KJV). It says: "Therefore I say unto you, **What things soever ye desire**, when ye pray, believe that ye receive them, and **ye shall have them**." This is who our God is. He not only sees our desires, needs, and wants but also wants to fulfill them. And even more critical, this scripture unlocks God's perfect system of faith that will enable us to receive everything He has for us. All it takes to operate in this incredible and free gift is the willingness to understand it.

DEFINING FAITH

The system of faith has its foundation in God's very nature as a generous and benevolent giver. As soon as we recognize this nature, we can begin our understanding of faith.

According to the dictionary, faith is "something that is believed especially with strong conviction," and "belief and trust in and loyalty to God." While this gives us a general idea of the concept of faith, I don't think it's the most accurate representation of how we can implement it in our lives. That's when we turn to the Bible. One of the most heavily quoted definitions of faith is found in Hebrews 11:1 (KJV). It says: "Now faith is the substance of things hoped for, the evidence of things not seen." Simple enough. So, that's faith. The substance of things hoped for and the evidence of things not seen. Crystal clear. Except I don't know about you, but that's still a little confusing at first glance. What does it mean that faith is the substance and the evidence? We'll get to that in a little while, but first, I think there's an even simpler definition that helps to build a stronger foundation to understanding faith.

Let's look at a story in John 20:24-29 (KJV):

> "But Thomas, one of the twelve, called Didymus, was not with them when Jesus came. The other disciples therefore said unto him, We have seen the Lord. But he said unto them, Except I shall see in his hands the print of the nails, and put my finger into the print of the nails, and thrust my hand into his side, I will not believe. And after eight days again his disciples were within, and Thomas with them: then came Jesus, the doors being shut, and stood in the midst, and said, Peace be unto you. Then saith he to Thomas, Reach hither thy finger, and behold my hands; and reach hither thy hand, and thrust it into my side: **and be not faithless, but believing.**"

At this moment, Thomas is talking to the disciples about a moment they experienced where Jesus came to them. Thomas chose not to believe what they were saying because he had not witnessed this moment himself. Eight days later, Jesus again went to the disciples, and this time, Thomas was there to witness it. The key part to this scripture that contributes to our definition of faith is the last thing Jesus says, "be not **faithless**, but **believing**." Here, Jesus is freely exchanging faith and belief as synonyms. If the opposite of being faithless is to be believing, then faith is the same thing as belief.

> FAITH IS SIMPLY WHAT YOU BELIEVE

This is just one example of Jesus using the words faith and belief interchangeably. In Matthew 9:27-29, we find a similar situation:

"And when Jesus departed thence, two blind men followed him, crying, and saying, Thou son of David, have mercy on us. And when he was come into the house, the blind men came to him: and Jesus saith unto them, **Believe** ye that I am able to do this? They said unto him, Yea, Lord. Then touched he their eyes, saying, According to your **faith** be it unto you."

Here, the blind men approached Jesus for healing. He responded with a question that asked if they believed that He was able to do so and then later tells them it was according to their faith that it be done. Throughout the New Testament, you will find countless examples of Jesus using faith and belief interchangeably. This leads to an extremely simple definition. Faith is simply what you believe. That's it. It's just what you believe.

What's crazy is that we use faith every day in areas of our lives that have nothing to do with spirituality. We use it in very practical situations. For example, if you tell me you will meet me in a particular place at a specific time, I use an element of faith to step out and be at that place at that time. Why? Because I believe you'll be there. When we take a physical step, we believe the floor will hold us. When we go to use our phone, we believe it will work.

We make assumptions based on our understanding, and those are our beliefs. It's faith. It's that simple: when you believe, you have faith. We don't typically use the word faith in daily life, because of its spiritual connotations, but we can always use it interchangeably with belief. There is an aspect of faith in almost everything we encounter.

THE LAW OF FAITH

The definition of faith, as we've established, is what you believe. Just as important to acknowledge is its nature. Romans 3:27 (KJV) says, "Where is boasting then? It is excluded. By what law? of works? Nay: but by **the law of faith**." Through this scripture, we see that faith is not just a concept but a law. It is the system designed to receive every desire and need that you have.

A law is a fact. A system that's always in effect regardless of your belief in it. The most obvious example of a law is gravity. From the moment that we wake up to the moment we go to sleep, and every other moment in between, gravity is at work. It's constant, keeping us tethered to the ground. Though we might not always notice or acknowledge its impacts, it's still there.

In the same way that gravity works, so does faith. Mark 11:24 (KJV) says this: "Therefore I say unto you, What things soever ye desire, when ye pray, believe that ye receive them, and ye shall have them." Faith is what we believe, but this scripture reveals the law of faith. It is a system designed by God to work the same way with the same results every single time, regardless of what you believe for. We start with a desire; we believe we receive it, and then we will have it. We'll cover the specifics of this as we move forward, but for now, I can't stress the importance of the concept of faith being a law. This is how faith works. Every. Single. Time. When you can understand and implement this system of faith, you will be able to obtain every promise you seek. Because God has prescribed a set of laws that govern everything and everyone in the realm of our reality, we have continual access to utilize those laws.

Just like gravity, faith is always at work. As we'll talk about in the coming chapters, what we believe cannot be based on what we can see. This is why it is so essential to understand the nature of faith. Because it is a law, it is always in operation. Even if we don't see it, it's still working, and it's not going away. It's constant.

WHY WALK IN FAITH?

Now that we know the definition and nature of faith, we need to address why we need it. Why should we even use faith at all? In a practical sense, we have to use faith to function. If we started questioning every belief we have, we would be paralyzed by doubt and worry, even in the smallest details. For example, say you decided to question your belief about gravity. You wouldn't even be able to take a step or pour yourself a cup of coffee without wondering, "Will this stuff start floating away?" Or worse: "Will I start floating away?" Faith is what tethers us (literally, in some cases) to the reality that we exist in. Faith, in a practical sense, is fundamental to our stability.

Even more important, though, is faith when it comes to walking with God. A closer look at the Bible makes you realize that there's so much more to faith than just receiving things that you desire. Hebrews 11:6 (KJV) says, "But without **faith** it is impossible to please him: for he that cometh to God must **believe** that he is, and that he is a rewarder of them that diligently seek him." Here we see another example of faith and belief used interchangeably, and we see that it is physically impossible to please God without faith. I don't know about you, but my greatest desire in life is to live a life pleasing to Him. If it is impossible to do that without faith, I want to make sure I understand and use it as much as possible.

2 Corinthians 5:7 (KJV) tells us: "(For we walk by faith, not by sight:)" This reveals that faith is more than just something we use, but something we live by. We move forward by using faith; it is our activation. We can't walk by what we see; we can only walk by what we believe. In Ephesians 6:16 (KJV), Paul says: "Above all, taking the shield of faith,

wherewith ye shall be able to quench all the fiery darts of the wicked." Here we see that faith is literally a weapon against the enemy and any attack that he might try to bring.

We please God with our faith; we walk by our faith; we protect ourselves with faith. None of those Scriptures contain any other qualifiers — it is through faith, and faith alone, that we can accomplish any of these things. Faith is absolutely crucial to our walk as believers.

In order to ever operate in faith, we have to understand what it is. As we've discovered, faith is what we believe. It's a law that is constant. It's how we please God, how we walk, and how we protect ourselves. Faith is the key to unlocking everything you've been seeking in life. As we dive deeper into the principles of faith, remember that faith begins with your willingness to understand and utilize it. As you do both of those things, I know you'll begin to see God move in a mighty way in your life.

CHAPTER TWO
WHERE FAITH BEGINS

Now that we've established the fundamentals of faith, we can begin to dive deeper into utilizing this eternal system to obtain God's promises. We've spent time developing an understanding of what faith is and why we should utilize it, but there is still so much to bring into view before we can see the full picture of faith. For instance, where does faith come from? How do we get it? Where does faith go once we get it? These questions are fundamental, and we'll start by answering the very first one: where does faith come from?

If faith is defined as what we believe, where do those beliefs come from? What's interesting is that all beliefs we have, whether practical or spiritual, stem from the same place. Romans 10:17 (KJV) tells us, "So then faith cometh by hearing, and hearing by the word of God." As this scripture reveals, faith comes by hearing.

Let's first take a look at faith coming by hearing in a practical sense. I'm willing to bet that you have a phone somewhere in the space you're in right now. Whether you're as technologically advanced as my two teenagers (pray for me, they know far too much) or are just generally aware of the features it has, you have a basic level of trust that your phone is going to work. Let's take it a step further and say that you have faith in your phone. You believe that if someone calls you right now, you can pick it up and have a conversation with them (again, unless you're like one of my teenagers who much prefer texting). My question is, where did that belief come from? Were we born with the knowledge of phone calls and texting and little yellow people that describe our moods? Don't tell anyone, but cell phones weren't even an idea when I was born, much less in existence. Meaning it would have been impossible for me to develop that belief from birth. The faith I have in my phone, and the same that you have in yours, came from hearing. Maybe not because we attended a class, read a book about it, or understood every inner-working part, but because we gained information about phones and considered that information valid enough to act upon.

This is how faith, on a spiritual level, works too. Consider this: what is the one act of faith that every Christian has in common? The answer is salvation. The most basic and universal example of faith is believing that Jesus died on the cross for our sins and confessing Him as our Lord and Savior so that we can live with Him forever in Heaven. The billions of testimonies that have walked the face of the Earth will reveal that this belief was not something that we were all born with.

So, where did it come from? For some, it was a miraculous moment of someone speaking an inspiring and convicting message. Others might say it came from their parents or grandparents instilling the truth of the Word from a young age. Maybe it was through a desperate attempt to find an answer to fill the void in their life that they frantically opened the pages of the Bible and found their solution in Jesus. It could've been a friend reaching out, a Facebook post, or a random encounter on the side of the road. Quite honestly, I could fill the rest of this book with ways people came to find their faith in God, but it's unnecessary. Because despite how we all heard about the gospel of Jesus, it was the hearing that enabled us to operate in its truth. Faith, even at its most basic level, comes by hearing.

> FAITH, EVEN AT ITS MOST BASIC LEVEL, COMES BY HEARING

And faith doesn't just stop after we get saved. In fact, that's just the beginning. Because if faith comes by hearing and hearing by the Word of God, as Romans 10:17 told us, that means we can believe for every promise that the Bible has to offer. Salvation is one of the thousands of things that the Bible says we can have. Just like we can believe that Jesus died on the cross for our sins, we can also believe that He's our Healer. We can believe He wants us to walk in increase and that He wants to give us peace. The list could go on forever. Basically, if you can find it in the Word, you can have it through faith. But it all comes down to one thing: hearing.

It's important to note that "hearing" doesn't always refer to the physical sense of picking up sound with our ears. We don't have to hear with our ears to have faith. If that were the case, there would be many people in the world who would be disqualified from even accessing faith. But that's not the case at all. In fact, Romans 10:17 (NIV) says, "Consequently, faith comes from hearing the message, and the message is heard through the word about Christ." This shows us that faith is not birthed from the action of hearing but the subject of hearing.

> FAITH IS NOT BIRTHED FROM THE ACTION OF HEARING, BUT THE SUBJECT OF HEARING

That subject, the birthplace of our faith, is the Word of God. Throughout the Bible, there are two Greek words used to describe the Word of God: Logos and Rhema. Logos is the written Word or the Bible. This encompasses any promise you see written between Genesis and Revelation. Rhema, on the other hand, is the spoken Word of God, more specifically those things that He communicates directly to your heart. Examples of Rhema might be things related to your calling, dreams, purposes, or plans for your life. Whether you read about a promise in the Bible or God spoke to your heart, what you heard becomes the starting point of your faith.

ACCEPTING THE WORD

I live in Florida and have for many years. One of the best parts of living in Florida is being able to go to the beach. You'll often find my family and I hanging out on the sandy shores with snacks, sunscreen, fishing poles, and surfboards. During the summers, we are there at least once a week.

You've probably never heard this before, but one of the craziest things about the beach, at least here in Florida, is that there are certain days where the water turns purple. Not just a bluish-purple either, like fluorescent purple. I know it sounds a little crazy, but I've had days at the beach where the water was literally so purple that it dyed the sand purple too. You're probably curious how it happens; I was too. So I did some research. According to an article I found on Google, there are particular and specific algae in the water in our area that turn purple during the summer, thus causing the water to reflect that same hue. If I'm remembering correctly, the change in color is supposed to be a defense mechanism against another type of algae that tries to take over the purple-producing species. However it happens, it's absolutely beautiful to see, and it's fascinating.

I mean, it would be if any of that last paragraph were true. Admittedly, I have never been to a beach and seen fluorescent purple water that stains the sand purple. I don't even know if that type of algae exists. My apologies for not telling the truth, but I wanted to illustrate a point. What went through your mind when I said that we have purple beaches here in Florida? Did you believe me? Was there any part of you that thought, "that's not true" or "I've never heard of that happening"? What happened was this: you heard something and then you had a choice. You could do one of two things: accept what I was saying and believe it to be true or reject what I was saying and believe it to be false. What this reveals is that there is more to faith than just hearing. There is an action on our part that determines if faith can take root in our lives and produce the fruit of that belief.

There's a parable that Jesus shares in the Bible that demonstrates this even further. Let's look at Mark 4:14-20 (NKJV), where it says:

> "The sower sows the word. And these are the ones by the wayside where the word is sown. When they hear, Satan comes immediately and

takes away the word that was sown **in their hearts**. These likewise are the ones sown on stony ground who, when they hear the word, immediately receive it with gladness; and they have no root in themselves, and so endure only for a time. Afterward, when tribulation or persecution arises for the word's sake, immediately they stumble. Now these are the ones sown among thorns; they are the ones who hear the word, and the cares of this world, the deceitfulness of riches, and the desires for other things entering in choke the word, and it becomes unfruitful. **But these are the ones sown on good ground, those who hear the word, accept *it*, and bear fruit:** some thirtyfold, some sixty, and some a hundred."

As you saw before in the purple ocean example, and as Jesus reveals in this parable, hearing is not the only key to having faith. Faith is activated the moment we hear the Word of God, but it is our response that determines its ability to stay activated. Once we hear, we either understand and accept what we have heard or reject and abandon it.

In Jesus' parable in Mark 4, He paints a picture of how people receive the seed of the Word and what happens after it has been sown. I first want to take a close look at verse 15, where it says: "And these are the ones by the wayside where the word is sown. When they hear, Satan comes immediately and takes away the word that was sown **in their hearts**." It's important to acknowledge that faith begins in our hearts. That's what Jesus was saying in this verse. Faith comes by hearing the Word, and the Word which we hear is sown in our hearts. It's important to note that our decision and action of faith is taken in the heart. It is not enough to just know something, we must believe. Faith is a heart action. Romans 10:10 (NIV) tells us, "**For it is with your heart that you believe** and are justified, and it is with your mouth that you profess your faith and are saved." The vehicle to our belief is our heart.

If we continue reading the parable, we see all the options we have when the Word is sown in our hearts (which is just a fancy way of saying we hear the Word). Throughout the parable, Jesus is explaining all the ways that the seed of the Word fails to produce any fruit. More specifically, what happens when the Word is heard but not accepted. We'll spend the entire next chapter looking at those examples in-depth, but here we're going to look at the one "success story." Verse 20 says this: "But these are the ones sown on good ground, those who **hear the word, accept** *it*, and **bear fruit**..." In this verse, we find the golden ticket to taking what we hear and turning it into what we believe: accepting. Our response to what we hear is what determines whether it becomes our belief or not. If we accept the Word to be true, it becomes the foundation for our faith at that moment and in the future. When the Word is sown on good ground, it is heard, accepted, and able to bear fruit.

> OUR RESPONSE TO WHAT WE HEAR IS WHAT DETERMINES WHETHER IT BECOMES OUR BELIEF OR NOT

Let's look back at my purple ocean example. When you first read that, did you believe it to be true? Whether you believed me or not, your response was based on two factors: knowledge and reliability. Knowledge, as in information and experience that you already have through personal interaction with the subject. Reliability, as in how much you trust me as the author of this book. If you also live in Florida or close to a beach and have never personally experienced a purple ocean or even heard of one, you probably read through that paragraph with a lot of confusion. Your knowledge determined whether or not you could believe what I was saying or not. On the other hand, you might never have personally experienced a purple ocean, but your level of trust in me as an author was strong enough to help you look past the uncertainty of the idea and believe that it's true. Whether you believed me or thought I was crazy, your knowledge of the situation and the reliability of the source helped you determine your action.

It's the same thing when we hear the Word of God. If we're honest, some promises in the Word of God are so profound that they can seem as unbelievable as a purple ocean. But, it is our knowledge of the reliability of the source of the Word that makes all the difference. The most important part of accepting any truth is considering its source to be reliable, and it is through knowledge that we can come to that conclusion. To set the record straight, every promise in the Word is true. One of my favorite verses, because it illustrates the constant validity of our God, is Numbers 23:19 (KJV), where it says: "God is not a man, that he should lie; neither the son of man, that he should repent: hath he said, and shall he not do it? or hath he spoken, and shall he not make it good?" Every Word written in the Bible is a word direct from the heart of our God. He cannot lie, and He cannot not follow through on His promises.

> EVERY WORD WRITTEN IN THE BIBLE IS A WORD DIRECT FROM THE HEART OF GOD

You should note that it might take time to develop the knowledge and the capacity that knowledge produces to be aware of the reliability of the Word. But notice I didn't say that knowledge produces the ability to believe. That's because it doesn't. Knowledge of the Word provides a better understanding of who God is and how He operates, making it easier to trust what He says. When it comes down to it, it is not how much you know, but rather how much you trust in what you know. Knowledge must confirm the value you place on what you hear for it to produce any fruit in your life. Accumulation of knowledge of the Word, specifically time in the Word, does not produce faith, but it does confirm God's character. The more you know about His promises and faithfulness, the easier it is to trust in His ability to fulfill your own desires.

QUALITY OVER QUANTITY

Question: if faith comes by hearing, then will more hearing produce more faith? The answer? Not necessarily. The Bible does not quantify the amount of hearing that faith requires; it just says faith comes by hearing. This means that you can hear the Word just once and have all the faith that you need to produce a promise in your life. The Gospels confirm this with multiple examples of one-time hearers who received incredible miracles. Perhaps one of the most well-known is the Roman Centurion. Let's take a closer look at this story in Matthew 8:5-10 (KJV):

> "And when Jesus was entered into Capernaum, there came unto him a centurion, beseeching him, And saying, Lord, my servant lieth at home sick of the palsy, grievously tormented. And Jesus saith unto him, I will come and heal him. The centurion answered and said, Lord, I am not worthy that thou shouldest come under my roof: but speak the

word only, and my servant shall be healed. For I am a man under authority, having soldiers under me: and I say to this man, Go, and he goeth; and to another, Come, and he cometh; and to my servant, Do this, and he doeth it. When Jesus heard it, he marvelled, and said to them that followed, **Verily I say unto you, I have not found so great faith, no, not in Israel."**

Here's another question for you: how many times did the Roman Centurion hear of Jesus' ability to heal? According to what we just read, he only knew for sure when he asked Jesus if He could heal his servant, and He said yes. This means the Roman Centurion only heard one time, but had such pronounced faith that Jesus marveled and declared to everyone around Him that he had great faith. How could someone who only heard once have such great faith that even Jesus was impressed? The answer is that the quality of hearing far outweighs the quantity. It didn't take the centurion knowing the ins and outs of how Jesus could do it, if He would do it, or even why He would do it. What's even more admirable is that the centurion didn't disqualify himself. He approached

Jesus with boldness, fully convinced that if He said He could heal his servant that there was no location too far that His healing power couldn't reach. The centurion asked, heard, and believed. And then we read His desire fulfilled in verse 13, "And Jesus said unto the centurion, Go thy way; and as thou hast believed, so be it done unto thee. And his servant was healed in the selfsame hour." In this instance, it did not take the centurion hearing over and over and over and over again to produce faith.

The same is true for you and me. The hearing that leads to faith only has to happen once. If there's one thing I've learned about faith, it's not something that can grow and stack. Faith is not a measurable substance that we can quantify and calculate. It is not the quantity of faith that produces the result, but the quality of the belief that you have. Even Jesus tells us this in Matthew 17:20 (MSG): "The simple truth is that if you had a mere kernel of faith, a poppy seed, say, you

> IT IS NOT THE QUANTITY OF FAITH THAT PRODUCES THE RESULT, BUT THE QUALITY OF BELIEF THAT YOU HAVE

would tell this mountain, 'Move!' and it would move. There is nothing you wouldn't be able to tackle."

And even if we look back to our Mark 4 parable about the sowing of the Word. Verse 24 (NKJV) tells us, "Then He said to them, '**Take heed what you hear. With the same measure you use, it will be measured to you**; and to you who hear, more will be given.'" The only measure that Jesus refers to when it comes to faith is the measure in which we approach our faith. It all comes down to what we hear and how much we decide to use what we hear.

Remember how I told you about God speaking to me? He told me that faith is not a container; it is an obtainer. Hearing the Word over and over again, for the sake of producing "more faith" is pointless. At the moment of hearing, faith comes. It's an instant exchange.

I say all of that also to say this: the quantity of hearing does not determine your ability to produce faith, but there is value to returning to what you heard to maintain your faith. In a perfect world, the exchange of faith would be instantaneous. We would hear, accept, believe, and receive within a moment, just like the Roman Centurion. As we'll talk about soon, however, there's this annoying little thing that sometimes even the strongest of beliefs have trouble standing up against: time. And not just time, but all of its equally annoying friends: troubles, trials, persecution, and problems. Guess what's even better about those annoying "little" things? They are coming specifically on assignment to steal the Word that you've heard. It's great news, I know.

The actual great news, though, is that the foundational understanding of faith that you are developing right now is what's going to give you the ability to withstand anything that comes to try to limit your ability to use it. When you recognize the process of faith and your responsibilities in operating the system, you become fully equipped to stand against any pressure designed to distract and deter you.

CHAPTER THREE
GOODBYE, FAITH

Have you ever been believing for something that didn't happen? If you have, you are not alone. If you haven't, you should probably be writing this book because you've got it figured out. All joking aside, I think we've all experienced disappointments or, at the very least, frustrations when believing God for something. And guess what? That's okay. None of your past failures disqualify you from trying again. In fact, let me tell you something that will set you free: you have never had a faith problem. If you believed for something and it didn't happen, it's not because you didn't have "enough" faith or "strong enough" faith. That's not the case at all. Faith has the same potential to succeed every time that it is activated for anyone who activates it. We have the same ability to walk in the very faith that Jesus did when He walked the Earth.

So if it's not my faith, what is it? The real problem is rejection and abandonment. If you have ever been believing for something and it didn't happen, I can guarantee that the issue comes down to either rejecting what you heard or abandoning it. And let me say one more thing before we look at these. Do not, I repeat, DO NOT feel bad if you have rejected or abandoned a belief. This is not to make you feel bad about past events, but rather equip you for future victories. We are all growing, every single day, don't let yesterday stop you from receiving all that tomorrow has to offer.

REJECTED, DENIED

In the last chapter, we talked specifically about the "success story" of Mark 4, namely hearing the Word, accepting it, and bearing fruit. What we didn't talk about were all the ways that beliefs can go wrong after hearing the Word. Let's take another look at the parable in Mark 4:14-20 (NKJV):

> "The sower sows the word. And these are the ones by the wayside where the word is sown. **When they hear, Satan comes immediately**

and takes away the word that was sown in their hearts. These likewise are the ones sown on stony ground who, **when they hear the word, immediately receive it** with gladness; and **they have no root in themselves**, and so endure only for a time. Afterward, **when tribulation or persecution arises** for the word's sake, **immediately they stumble**. Now these are the ones sown among thorns; they are the ones who **hear the word**, and the **cares of this world**, the **deceitfulness of riches**, and the **desires for other things** entering in **choke the word**, and **it becomes unfruitful**. But these are the ones sown on good ground, those who hear the word, accept it, and bear fruit: some thirtyfold, some sixty, and some a hundred."

The first example Jesus uses is the seed sown by the wayside (note that the wayside simply means the edge of a road). Verse 15 says:

"And these are the ones by the wayside where the word is sown. **When they hear**, Satan comes **immediately** and **takes away** the word that was **sown in their hearts.**"

Matthew 13:18-19 (NKJV), which reiterates the parable of the sower, says this:

> "Therefore hear the parable of the sower: When anyone hears the word of the kingdom, and does not understand it, then the wicked one comes and snatches away what was sown in his heart. This is he who received seed by the wayside."

Those who hear on the wayside are those who hear but aren't able to understand what they hear. In those cases, Satan comes immediately and steals the Word – meaning the faith it could have produced is literally dead on arrival. To accept, you must first understand. What you do not understand, Satan comes immediately and steals. This is the first pitfall you have to avoid: rejection.

Anytime you hear something but don't accept it, whether it's because you don't understand it or blatantly choose not to accept it, you reject it. Rejection is dangerous because it disqualifies the activation of faith immediately. If you cannot agree with and accept the Word, you reject its potential to produce in your life.

Say that I had a friend named Bob. Bob was in pressing need of a raise at work. He's reading the Bible one day and sees Ephesians 3:20 (KJV) that says, "Now unto him that is able to do exceeding abundantly above all that we ask or think, according to the power that worketh in us." After reading the scripture, Bob thinks about it for a minute. He starts asking himself all these questions: "why would God ever do exceedingly in this situation?", and "I don't know how I could get a raise, is that even possible?" Bob tries, but he just can't understand how God could do something like that in his life. Because Bob couldn't comprehend that promise from God, he rejected it. At that moment, his ability to receive what the Bible told him he could have is instantly voided. Rejection renders the Word impotent, which, in turn, destroys the faith it could have produced.

> REJECTION RENDERS THE WORD IMPOTENT, WHICH, IN TURN, DESTROYS THE FAITH IT COULD HAVE PRODUCED

But I'm not just here to bring doom and gloom with no solution. The key to overcoming rejection is developing an understanding of the Word. When you realize that a lack of understanding could limit your ability to receive faith, it becomes all the more important to build your understanding. In 2 Timothy 2:15 (KJV), it tells us to **"Study to shew thyself approved unto God, a workman that needeth not to be ashamed, rightly dividing the word of truth."** This is how we understand the Word. It doesn't require a doctorate in theology, 24 hours a day and seven days a week spent locked in a prayer closet, or even a lifetime devoted to ministry. Developing an understanding of the Word just means that you spend time in the Word, and you spend time with God in His presence through prayer and worship.

We spend time with God so we can understand Him. The value of that time is priceless because your understanding unlocks the full potential of your faith. You can facilitate faith's inception in your life by being a conscious, determined student of the Word of God. The more you study, the more you will understand. The more you understand, the less you will reject, and the more you will accept. The more you accept, the more your faith

> YOU CAN FACILITATE FAITH'S INCEPTION IN YOUR LIFE BY BEING A CONSCIOUS, DETERMINED STUDENT OF THE WORD OF GOD

will flourish. You cannot apply faith to your circumstances unless faith is a resource you can draw from – it has to be present inside of you. Faith isn't something that comes from an external source when you have a time of crisis. It doesn't fall from the sky in moments of desperation. Faith begins the moment you hear, understand, and accept the truth and promises of the Word.

ABANDONMENT ISSUES

As the parable continues in Mark 4:16-17 (NKJV), it says this:

> "These likewise are the ones sown on stony ground who, **when they hear the word**, immediately **receive it with gladness**; and they have **no root** in themselves, and so endure only for a time. Afterward, when **tribulation or persecution** arises for the word's sake, immediately they **stumble**."

As we see through this example, sometimes, the beginning of faith seems promising but doesn't ever take root to produce the promise. When Jesus is talking about the seed sown on the stony ground, He says those people hear the Word, immediately receive it, but then when trouble comes, they stumble. In this case, when the Word was heard, it was received, and it was received with gladness. Rejection is not the issue. But we go on to read that even though the Word wasn't rejected, it still didn't produce a promise. After some time, when tribulation or persecution comes, and specifically for the Word's sake, they immediately stumble. In this example, Jesus is not referring to a rejection issue, but an abandonment issue. When the Word was sown to these people, they heard it, understood it, and they were even excited about it. But it didn't last through the trouble that came for it.

Let's take a closer look at this scripture in the Message version. Mark 4:16-17 (MSG) says this:

> "And some are like the seed that lands in the gravel. When they first hear the Word, they respond with great enthusiasm. **But there is such shallow soil of character** that when the emotions wear off and some difficulty arrives, there is nothing to show for it."

The lack of ability to maintain the belief results in abandonment of it.

Let's put this in terms of our friend Bob who was believing for a raise at work. In this case, Bob comes across Ephesians 3:20, where it says God can do exceedingly and abundantly, and Bob is pumped. It's the answer he's been looking for! He reads the Word, accepts it in His heart, and is walking in faith. He walks into work the next day, completely excited because he believes God is going to do exceedingly and abundantly in his life, and he's going to get a raise.

Within minutes of walking into work, Bob's boss randomly calls him into her office. He practically jumps out of his chair because this is the moment he's been waiting for. As soon as he gets in the office, his boss begins to express frustration about a project he had been working on. Bob instantly deflates. There's nothing positive that comes from the meeting, and there's definitely no raise. He spends the rest of the day completely upset that God didn't do exceedingly and abundantly in his life, and he stops believing that He will. Just as quickly as Bob heard the promise and activated his faith, he let it go.

In this scenario, Bob understood what the Word was saying, he accepted it, and he believed it. But Bob could not sustain through the tribulation and persecution that came for what he was believing.

Obviously, this is a made-up example, but I think we've all experienced moments where what we expect doesn't happen right away (or on our timeline), and we become discouraged and disappointed. It is in those moments that we have to determine whether we will abandon our belief or maintain it.

The good news is that there is something that we can use to combat abandonment, but before we get to it, let's keep reading the Mark 4 parable. Verses 18-19 give us another example of a faith failure; there it says,

> "Now these are the ones sown among thorns; they are the ones who **hear the word**, and the **cares of this world**, the **deceitfulness of riches**, and the **desires for other things** entering in **choke the word**, and **it becomes unfruitful.**"

In this example, Jesus explains that there are even more things that are going to try to come against the Word so that we are unable to operate in faith. The Message version says it even better:

> "The seed cast in the weeds represents the ones who hear the kingdom news but are

overwhelmed with worries about all the things they have to do and all the things they want to get. The stress strangles what they heard, and nothing comes of it."

If we were classifying the root of this issue, I would say that it's both a rejection and abandonment problem. In this case, the Word is heard, but worry and stress come and strangle what was heard so that there can be no harvest. The potential of faith is robbed as the hearer rejected what was heard for fear of the process it would take to receive it. In this case, it is the enormity of the truth that makes the pursuit of its manifestation overwhelming and unattractive.

Whether it is tribulation and persecution, cares of the world, the deceitfulness of riches, or desires for other things, these two examples reveal that there are things actively pursuing your faith. And not in a good way. These things are intentionally coming to separate you from the potential that your faith can produce, and you must be ready to stand up to them.

But as I said, there is a key that enables you to do so. That key is value. More specifically, the value you place on the Word that you hear. Just like the more you understand the Word, the less you reject it;

the more you value the Word, the less you abandon it. To put it in practical terms, it's like buying a new car. In most cases, when you buy a new car, the amount you spend is the most amount of money that will ever be paid for it. As much as it's worth at that moment, it's value immediately declines when you drive away from the dealership. The wear and tear that happens from day-to-day driving also decrease its value. In the sense of a material object like a car, the value is finite, so a decrease is understandable. But the value of the Word is infinite. It never loses an ounce of its truth or validity.

> THE WORD IS NEVER AFFECTED BY DAY-TO-DAY WEAR AND TEAR; ITS VALUE IS NEVER-CHANGING, NEVER-ENDING, AND ALWAYS PRESENT

You'll notice that in the parable, Jesus doesn't say that the Word sown on the stony ground lost its truth; instead, it was that the heart that received it could not maintain the belief that it was true. The Word is never affected by day-to-day wear and tear; its value is never-changing, never-ending, and always present. Just like spending time in the Word produces a better understanding; a greater understanding of the Word produces a greater value. The value that you place on the Word is directly related to the fruition of your promise. Mark 4:24 (AMP) tells us:

> "Pay attention to what you hear. By your own standard of measurement [that is, **to the extent that you study spiritual truth and apply godly wisdom] it will be measured to you [and you will be given even greater ability to respond]**—and more will be given to you besides."

How you approach the Word will determine its impact on your life and the production of your faith. The value that you place on it, despite and in the middle of trouble and trials, will determine the promises that you see come to pass and those that you allow to be taken.

> HOW YOU APPROACH THE WORD WILL DETERMINE ITS IMPACT ON YOUR LIFE

OUT OF SIGHT, OUT OF MIND?

In addition to valuing the Word, we can also fight against abandonment through our perception. One of the most important things that you need to understand about faith is that it often takes time (and sometimes *a lot* of it) to see what you're believing for come to pass. As much as I would like to tell you as soon as we believe, we have what we're believing for in our hands; I can't lie to you (except about the purple ocean thing… Sorry about that again, it was just to illustrate a point).

The thing about faith is that it's God's system, and I don't know if you've noticed, but God doesn't do things how we do things. His ways are higher and greater, and well let's face it, they're typically a lot longer. The Bible says in 2 Peter 3:8 (MSG), "With God, one day is as good as a thousand years, a thousand years as a day." And yes, sometimes from the moment we believe for something to the moment we see it fulfilled, it feels like a thousand years. But verse 9 reminds us, "God isn't late with his promise as some measure lateness." When it comes to faith, we have to understand that things don't always work like we think they're going to work. But, and this is a big one, that doesn't mean they're not working. God is never a day late or a dollar short on the promises that you believe for.

Now, I'd also be lying if I told you this was just as easily done as it is said. That's not the case either.

In fact, those times where we have released faith and have done everything "right," and we have yet to see our promise fulfilled are some of the most challenging moments we can face as believers. The waiting period often feels like the worst period, but it's never a wasted period. And while we wait for our promise, with troubles and trials continually coming at us, we have to learn how to exist outside of what we feel and see.

> THE WAITING PERIOD OFTEN FEELS LIKE THE WORST PERIOD, BUT IT'S NEVER A WASTED PERIOD

The Bible tells us in 2 Corinthians 5:7 (AMP): "for we walk by faith, not by sight [living our lives in a manner consistent with our confident belief in God's promises]—" This is the key to withstanding the waiting. We have to walk by faith and not by sight. Walking by sight just means that we live and make our decisions based on our senses, which are influenced by the tangible. It means we look for what we can feel and see to determine if our faith is working or not. But the Bible calls us to walk by faith. To be guided by the understanding and value that we have in the truth of the Word. This means we have to be influenced by and convinced of the intangible nature of faith and the promises it's producing.

There's a story in the Bible that highlights the importance of walking by faith and not by sight. We read in Mark 11:12-14 (MSG):

> "As they left Bethany the next day, he [Jesus] was hungry. Off in the distance he saw a fig tree in full leaf. He came up to it expecting to find something for breakfast, but found nothing but fig leaves. (It wasn't yet the season for figs.) He addressed the tree: "No one is going to eat fruit from you again—ever!" And his disciples overheard him."

After this happened, Jesus and His disciples continued to Jerusalem. They did what they were there to do, and the next morning passed by the same fig tree that Jesus had cursed the day before. We read in verses 20-21:

> "In the morning, walking along the road, they saw the fig tree, shriveled to a dry stick. Peter, remembering what had happened the previous day, said to him, 'Rabbi, look—the fig tree you cursed is shriveled up!'"

Look at what happened when Jesus cursed the fig tree. The second He cursed it, it died at its root. Yet it still looked alive. The leaves were still green, the branch was still sturdy, and the tree's appearance would have told you that it was completely alive. But Jesus' act of faith made that fig tree die instantly. Jesus then goes on to give us another foundational key to understanding faith in verse 24. The King James Version says, "Therefore I say unto you, What things soever ye desire, when ye pray, believe that ye receive them, and ye shall have them."

The picture of the fig tree is what happens when we believe we receive when we pray. We may not see instant results in the natural realm – the outward appearance of the fig tree – but we instantly receive what we have believed in the spiritual realm – the root of the fig tree is dead. It may take time to manifest so we can see it in the natural, but what we have believed has, in fact, already been accomplished. This is what it means to walk by faith and not by sight.

The more you learn about faith, the more you will see how important it is to hold on to and value the Word. Spend time developing an understanding of the Word so that you can fully value the Word and overcome the trials, troubles, and time that it takes to produce its promises. Ultimately, if you can live outside of what you see and feel and live only by your faith, choosing not to reject or abandon your beliefs, you will see the desires of your heart come to pass.

CHAPTER FOUR
SUBSTANCE & EVIDENCE

Often when I preach about faith at a church, whether it is my own or one that I am visiting, I ask the people a question. I say, "What is faith?" And then I'll pause. Those brave enough to answer will often throw out a lot of different definitions all at the same time. Typically, the answer that I'm looking for is "what you believe," because as we have previously covered, that's what faith is. But one of the most common answers I get when I ask that question is, "the substance of things hoped for, the evidence of things not seen." While that is not the answer that I'm looking for at the moment, it is a right answer. The Bible tells us in Hebrews 11:1-3 (KJV):

"Now faith is the substance of things hoped for, the evidence of things not seen. For by it the elders obtained a good report. Through faith we understand that the worlds were framed by the word of God, so that things which are seen were not made of things which do appear."

Now, you might be thinking, "if the Bible says faith is the substance of things hoped for and the evidence of things not seen, why did you tell me that faith is what I believe?" The answer is that faith is both. To understand and build a development of faith, we needed to look at it from a practical and simplified angle. Faith being what you believe reveals an action, it tells us our responsibility. But the biblical definition that we just read in Hebrews 11:1 reveals the nature of faith; it tells us what faith does.

HOPE AND FAITH

Before we break down this scripture even further, let's take a minute and talk about the difference between hope and faith. As we can see in Hebrews 11:1, *faith* is the substance of things *hoped* for. One of the greatest misconceptions I see about faith is that people think that hope and faith are the same things. They are not. In fact, it's dangerous to think they are the same thing, because they fulfill very different, specific, and important roles individually.

The dictionary definition for hope is: "to desire with expectation of obtainment or fulfillment." The Bible tells us in Hebrews 6:19 (AMP),

> **"This hope [this confident assurance]** we have as an anchor of the soul [it cannot slip and it cannot break down under whatever pressure bears upon it]—a safe and steadfast hope that enters within the veil [of the heavenly temple, that most Holy Place in which the very presence of God dwells],"

I love how hope is defined in this verse. As you can see above, it calls hope our confident assurance. I like to combine both the dictionary definition and the one we just read to define hope as confident expectation with joyful anticipation.

Now that we know what hope is let's talk about where hope comes from. Hope is found in the Word of God. I like to think of hope as the stepping stone from hearing to believing. When we read the Word and find a promise, our hope (or our confident expectation) is our response to the reality

HOPE IS FOUND IN THE WORD OF GOD

of that promise in our lives. For example, say you need healing for your body. You are desperate for an answer and solution. One day, you're reading the Bible, and you come across Isaiah 53:5 (KJV) that says, "But he was wounded for our transgressions, he was bruised for our iniquities: the chastisement of our peace was upon him; and with his stripes we are healed." At that moment, the Word brought hope. It gave you the confident expectation that you could be healed. But here's the thing, hope is not capable of producing that promise. You cannot just hope that by His stripes you will be healed.

This is why it's so important to differentiate between hope and faith. So often, people think they are operating in faith because they expect something to happen, but they've never properly formed the beliefs necessary to receive it. A huge difference between hope and faith is the tense they're in. Hope is in the future; faith is in the now.

> HOPE IS IN THE FUTURE; FAITH IS IN THE NOW

Hope believes it's going to happen. Faith believes it's happening now. Mark 11:24 (KJV) tells us, "Therefore I say unto you, What things soever ye desire, when ye pray, believe that ye receive them, and ye shall have them." Hope is later; faith is now. We see this also illustrated in Hebrews 11:1 (KJV), where it says: "NOW faith is..." Hope is how you stay connected to the promise, but it is not the obtainer that faith is to receive that promise.

Hope and faith work together to receive the promises of the Word. We need both to be able to form and sustain the beliefs required to operate the system of faith. Things hoped for don't change until faith materializes them, just as the desire that produces the faith isn't truly available without hope.

I like to think of hope as being the God-side; it's His promises that affirm our desires and give us the expectation needed to produce the beliefs. And I like to think of faith as the human side; it's our tool and responsibility to activate the hope in the promises to see them come to pass. I don't think we can have faith without first having hope, just as hope is useless without the action of faith. Faith is the activation of hope. It takes what we desire and turns it into what we can receive. Only faith can access what hope provided.

SUBSTANCE AND EVIDENCE

Understanding how hope and faith work together is pivotal for understanding those three verses we first read in Hebrews 11:1-3. Verse 1 specifically tells us that faith is the substance of things hoped for and the evidence of things not seen. I want to put an in-depth focus on those two things: the substance and the evidence.

Let's start with the first part. Faith is the substance of things hoped for. The definition of the word substance is "physical material from which something is made or which has discrete existence." Remember, when I told you how God spoke to me about faith being an obtainer? In essence, that is the nature of this part of faith. It is the substance of things hoped for, meaning faith is what you put in the exchange until it materializes the promise in the natural. Once you hear and accept a promise from the Word of God, you are in faith. That faith becomes the substance of those very things you have hope in and expectation for. That substance is the proof of things not yet seen that will eventually be revealed to your senses.

With that being said, I want to clarify that faith is not a tangible substance that you can touch and feel in your hand. It is a placeholder until it has obtained the promise that you are believing for. The faith itself is not the thing you are believing for, but it holds its place until that thing is produced. What's even better news is that the substance of faith, though not as tangible, is just as real as the promise you are believing for.

Perhaps a better way to explain this is to look at the next part of that verse, where it says that faith is the evidence of things not seen. This might sound confusing because how can you have evidence of something that's not seen? Let's first take a look at the definition of evidence. Evidence means "something that furnishes proof." In an even simpler definition, evidence is proof. And so, that's what faith is; it is the proof of things not yet seen. But what are those things? Basically, those things are anything in the unseen; what you're believing for, what's yet to come, the fulfillment of your dreams, you name it. Faith is the evidence of everything that we are yet to see in our lives.

Faith as a substance is a placeholder, whereas faith as evidence is a proof-producer. Faith produces the substance for hopes, and faith produces the evidence of the invisible. Faith is the material that produces your hopes and the factor that materializes the invisible. The one side is the substance that produces your hopes, and the other side is the evidence to produce the unseen.

> FAITH AS A SUBSTANCE IS A PLACEHOLDER, WHEREAS FAITH AS EVIDENCE IS A PROOF-PRODUCER

I want to look at Hebrews 11:1 (AMP) because it illustrates this idea of faith as the substance and evidence even further. There it says:

> "Now faith is the assurance (**title deed, confirmation**) of things hoped for (**divinely guaranteed**), and the evidence of things not seen [the conviction of their reality—faith comprehends as fact what cannot be experienced by the physical senses]."

When I first read this verse in the Amplified version, I got so excited because it gave me this revelation on the substance and evidence of faith that I'd never had before. I want you to pay close attention to that word "title deed" that is bolded above. As an extended definition of the word assurance (or the substance, as it is written in the King James Version), "title deed" gives the best example of how faith works.

Think about it like this. If you own a car or even any type of motor vehicle, you must also have a title. That title shows the registered owners, the make, model, and year number, along with the VIN, and any other relevant information about the car. What's crazy about the title is that one little piece of paper designates whether or not you possess the vehicle. In fact, you could have that same car sitting in your driveway, or you could be driving it around, but without that paper, it does not belong to you. Without the title, you don't own any car; but with it, the car doesn't even need to be present for you to own it.

This is what Hebrews 11:1 (AMP) means when it says faith is the title deed. Faith is your title to every promise written in the Word of God. It is the placeholder that denotes possession, even in the absence of what you are believing for. When you find a promise in the Word of God, and believe it, that faith becomes the title deed to whatever promise you are believing for. The Word of God and the specific promise you are believing for becomes the proof that it belongs to you.

Here's another way to look at it: if you walk on a piece of empty land and just claim it as your own, does that make the land yours? Absolutely not. You could walk on it as much as you want, tell all of your friends that it's yours, you could even put a building on it, but that land is not yours without the title deed. What this signals is that the paperwork for the land (or even the car) is more real than the land (or car) itself. Proof of ownership is more tangible than the actual object itself because it identifies possession. What this means in terms of faith is that the promises of the Word of God and the faith that can produce them are more real than the tangible objects themselves. Why? Because faith denotes possession, even with a lack of materialization. We can take away from this verse that faith, as both substance and evidence, gives proof producing ability to things that are not yet seen

> FAITH DENOTES POSSESSION, EVEN WITH A LACK OF MATERIALIZATION

THINGS NOT YET SEEN

Speaking of things "not yet seen," we need to take a moment to discuss the difference between the two realms at play when it comes to faith. Let's look back at the second half of Hebrews 11:1 (AMP). It says, "and the evidence of things not seen [the conviction of their reality—**faith comprehends as fact what cannot be experienced by the physical senses**]." As you can see, it says faith comprehends what cannot be experienced by the physical senses. Even in the King James Version, it tells us that faith is the evidence of things not seen. This tells me that there is a place where the promises we are believing for exist; we just aren't able to physically sense them. Let's look at 2 Corinthians 4:17-18 (TPT), where it says:

> "We view our slight, short-lived troubles in the light of eternity. We see our difficulties as the substance that produces for us an eternal, weighty glory far beyond all comparison, because we don't focus our attention on **what is seen** but on **what is unseen**. For **what is seen is temporary**, but the **unseen realm is eternal**."

This tells us that there are two realms: one that is seen and one that is unseen. The seen realm is the temporal. This is everything in the natural, the things that we can see and sense. It is the reality that we exist in and the condition of the Earth. Everything in the temporal is subject to change.

On the other hand, the unseen realm is the eternal. The eternal is the realm of God. This is everything in the spirit; the things we cannot tangibly see and sense. Here, God's systems operate, and so do the principles of the Kingdom. Eternal means it lasts forever. It is the nature of God and the condition of His Kingdom.

And while we exist in the natural, our nature as believers includes the eternal. 1 Corinthians 6:17 (KJV) tells us, "but he that is joined unto the Lord is one spirit." This means when we accept Jesus into our lives, we become one with Him in spirit. So while we might exist in a temporal realm and have a natural body and soul, our spirit is the eternal nature and DNA of God Himself. 2 Peter 1:3-4 (NKJV) confirms this by saying:

> "as His divine power has given to us all things that pertain to life and godliness, through the

> knowledge of Him who called us by glory and virtue, by which have been given to us exceedingly great and precious promises, that through these you may be partakers of the divine nature, having escaped the corruption that is in the world through lust."

Through His sacrifice on the cross for our sins, Jesus provided access to every promise we could ever desire. The Bible even says every promise is yes and amen in 2 Corinthians 1:20. Basically, we can be confident that when Jesus said "it is finished" with His final breath as He laid down His life for ours, He completed every promise that we will ever need or desire. He took care of everything.

BY GRACE

Through faith, we obtain these promises, but there's also another factor that is at play. Ephesians 2:8-9 (KJV) tells us, "For by grace are ye saved through faith; and that not of yourselves: it is the gift of God:" That second factor is grace. The Bible tells us in this scripture that by grace, we are saved through faith. Grace gave you access to everything you'll ever need in life, and faith allows you to access everything grace has ever provided you.

The best example is to look at your own salvation. When you asked Jesus into your life, did you know all of the incredible promises on the other side of your decision? Did you know that you could walk in complete healing, prosperity, and victory? Or did you make the decision because you needed a Savior? Because you needed redemption? While everyone's testimony is different, I can guarantee that you had no clue all of the incredible, or as that scripture we just read in 2 Peter 1:4 says, exceedingly great and precious promises that stood on the other side of your salvation. Here's another question: when were all of those promises made available to you? The answer is the moment that you accepted Jesus as your Lord and Savior.

> GRACE PROVIDED EVERYTHING YOU'RE EVER GOING TO NEED IN LIFE AT THE MOMENT OF YOUR SALVATION

Grace provided everything you're ever going to need in life at the moment of your salvation. That was the plan of God. At the very inception of our faith journey, salvation, we see the work of grace. It is by grace through faith that we experience redemption. But this interaction is not finished once you get saved. Every promise that you use faith to obtain is through the grace that has enabled it. Grace provides the promise; faith receives it. Everything you will ever need in life has already been completed through grace; then, it is our job to use our faith to receive it. Let's take a closer look at 2 Peter 1:3, but this time in the Passion Translation,

> "**Everything** we could **ever need** for life and complete devotion to God has **already** been deposited in us **by his divine power**. For all this was lavished upon us through the rich experience of knowing him who has called us by name and invited us to come to him through a glorious manifestation of his goodness."

In this scripture, we can see that Jesus' sacrifice and divine power have given us access to everything we could ever need.

For whatever you face in life, or whatever you desire, Jesus has already provided the promise you need to overcome or fulfill it in the Word of God. As I said before, He finished it all the moment that He gave His life on the cross. This means that Jesus doesn't have to get back up on the cross every time we need or believe for something. If we need healing, grace has already provided it. If we need financial provision, grace has already provided it. If we need restoration in our marriages or with our families, grace has already provided it. Whatever it is that we need, grace has already provided it.

When you understand the work of grace in your life, it becomes so much easier to operate in faith. At this point, it should be extremely clear that faith is not some mystic ideology that only the "elite members of Christianity" (which isn't a thing, by the way) can partake in. Faith is simply a tool that is of equal availability to every believer willing to use it.

Remember how we started this section off by talking about the differences between the temporal and the eternal? We focused so heavily on those because we need to understand how faith operates between the two realms. Ephesians 1:3 (AMP) says, "Blessed and worthy praise be the God and Father of our Lord Jesus Christ, who has blessed us with every **spiritual blessing in the heavenly realms** in Christ." Those exceedingly great and precious promises that grace provided us access to exist in the heavenly, or eternal realm. Everything we need exists in the eternal. And as you know by now, we exist in the temporal, in the natural realm. The vehicle to get the promises from the eternal into the temporal? You guessed it. Faith.

Faith is activated in the temporal but operates in the eternal. It goes into the unseen, eternal, heavenly realm and pulls every completed and perfect blessing into our seen, temporal, and natural realm.

FAITH IS ACTIVATED IN THE TEMPORAL BUT OPERATES IN THE ETERNAL

Hebrews 11:3 (MSG) sums it up perfectly by saying, "By faith, we see the world called into existence by God's word, **what we see created by what we don't see.**" This is what faith does. It manifests the completed promises of God into our temporary reality. So that everything we see is created by what we don't see. It is our faith that receives what grace has already provided, and it is our faith that stands in the gap of what we're believing for until it does manifest.

Until this point, we have spent our time developing an understanding of how to form faith, which is extremely important. But, it is not the only thing needed to receive the promises of God. Now that we understand how faith operates and where it operates, we can begin learning how to release faith. It's essential to keep in mind the nature of faith and our responsibility in using it as we move forward to release it. Know that whatever you are believing for, you are closer than you have ever been to receiving because you are learning about the intricacies of the powerful force of faith.

CHAPTER FIVE
RELEASING FAITH

Now that you have a foundational knowledge of faith, we can begin to discuss how to release faith. This step is pivotal for seeing your promises come to pass. In fact, releasing faith is the most **essential step to the entire process because faith is not just something that you have; it's something that you do.**

FAITH IN TWO PLACES

Until this point, we've learned about hearing the Word, accepting it, and believing. These are the essentials for forming faith and our beliefs. But believing is not just something that we do in one moment and then forget about, at least not if we expect to receive what we're believing for. When you believe, faith takes up residence in your life. Our next step to operating faith is releasing it. To do so, we have to first understand where faith exists.

Think about it this way: what's the most essential part of driving a car? Some people might think it's the car itself or maybe even gas. In reality, the most crucial part of driving a car is the car key. You can have every bit of knowledge on how a car works, why a car works, or even how to drive, but if you don't know where your car key is, you won't ever be able to use it. It's the same thing with faith. Understanding the location of faith helps you to operate the entire system and sustain it through the pressures that accompany the process.

I remember when I first got saved, even before I went to Bible School, I did a lot of studying. I would read my Bible for hours on end because I wanted to know as much as I could. I remember there was a season I was studying about faith, and I had all of these questions, some you've probably had before reading this book. What is faith? How does it work? What does it do? Where is faith? Why isn't my faith working? It was a few months later that all of a sudden, I heard the Lord say to me, "Faith is in two places. Faith is in the mouth, and faith is in the heart." That was the first time I had ever come across the idea that faith is in two places. At first, it didn't make total sense, but with that foundational knowledge, I began to study more, and I came across Romans 10:8-10 (AMP). There it says:

> "But what does it say? "The word is near you, in your mouth and in your heart"—that is, the word [the message, the basis] of faith which we preach — because if you acknowledge and confess with your mouth that Jesus is Lord [recognizing His power, authority, and majesty as God], and believe in your heart that God raised Him from the dead, you will be saved. For with the heart a person believes [in Christ as Savior] resulting in his justification [that is, being made righteous—being freed of the guilt of sin and made acceptable to God]; and with the mouth he acknowledges and confesses [his faith openly], resulting in and confirming [his] salvation."

These verses reveal where faith exists. Faith is found in your heart and your mouth. What does this mean? As we see in verse 10, and as we've already addressed when

FAITH IS FOUND IN YOUR HEART AND YOUR MOUTH

we talked about hearing and accepting the Word, you believe with your heart. Once you hear and accept, a belief is formed in your heart. But as verse 10 also reveals, there is a second step: you have to confess your beliefs with your mouth.

The most fundamental example of this forming and releasing of beliefs is found in your first step to faith as believers: when you got saved. Verse 9 tells us that whoever believes in their heart and confesses with their mouth will be saved. When you first asked Jesus into your life, you had to make the decision that you believed He was your Lord and Savior. But you didn't just believe that in your heart; you had to confess it with your mouth. You had to confirm your belief with words. I love how the Amplified version repeatedly says that with your mouth, you acknowledge and confess what you believe in your heart. If I'm honest, this is why this chapter is the most important in this book because without releasing your faith and understanding how to do so properly, your beliefs will never manifest.

THE PRAYER OF FAITH

I want to revisit a story that we read in Chapter Three. In Mark 11, we saw Jesus and His disciples coming across a fig tree on the way to a certain location. Jesus stopped by the fig tree and saw that it had no figs, so He cursed it. As far as the eye could see, the fig tree (at least at that moment) looked to be completely alive. In Chapter Three, we discussed the importance of walking by faith and not by sight because even though it didn't look dead instantly, it was dead the moment that Jesus cursed it. However, in light of releasing faith, I want to take a closer look at Mark 11:20-24 (KJV), as He and His disciples are on their way out of the town a few days later. Here's what it says:

> "And in the morning, as they passed by, they saw the fig tree dried up from the roots. And Peter calling to remembrance saith unto him, Master, behold, the fig tree which thou cursedst is withered away. And Jesus answering saith unto them, Have faith in God. For verily I say unto you, That whosoever shall say unto this mountain, Be thou removed, and be thou cast into the sea; and shall not doubt in his heart, but shall believe that those things which he saith shall come to pass; he shall have whatsoever he saith. Therefore I say

unto you, What things soever ye desire, when ye pray, believe that ye receive them, and ye shall have them."

I believe this is one of the most powerful moments in the Bible because it illustrates the entire faith process. Before we get to breaking that process down, I want to make a quick note. Something that always stuck out to me about this story was Jesus' reasoning for cursing the fig tree. We know that He cursed it because there were no figs on the tree, but verse 13 tells us why: "he found nothing but leaves; for the time of figs was not yet." This always confused me because Jesus obviously knew that it was not the time for figs to be in season. So if He knew that it wasn't the time for figs, why did He even go up to it in the first place? And even more, why would He curse a tree that was just existing in its normal process?

After years of wondering, one day, it finally clicked. I believe that Jesus cursing the fig tree was about one thing only: undeveloped faith. In this case, Jesus was addressing Peter and his seemingly surprised response that the fig tree had withered after Jesus cursed it. He took the opportunity to reveal the nature of faith to Peter. But, He also used it to illustrate it to us as well. Because ultimately, faith is not a work in progress after it's been released. It has to be processed before it's released, or else it won't be able to withstand the pressure. Your faith and its accompanying understanding must be completely developed before you release it. This is Jesus' entire purpose for cursing the fig tree: to reveal the value of developed faith, not just a belief in the promise, but a belief in the process.

> **YOUR FAITH AND ITS ACCOMPANYING UNDERSTANDING MUST BE COMPLETELY DEVELOPED BEFORE YOU RELEASE IT**

To understand that process, let's first look at verse 23. There it says,

> "For verily I say unto you, That whosoever shall say unto this mountain, Be thou removed, and be thou cast into the sea; and shall not doubt in his heart, but shall believe that those things which he saith shall come to pass; he shall have whatsoever he saith."

The first thing to acknowledge is that again we see the connection between forming faith in the heart and releasing it with the mouth. Jesus tells us that whosoever shall say and not doubt in the heart but believe, can have whatever he says. This is the formula that Jesus gives us for faith. We can literally obtain anything when we follow this process.

I want to take a moment and talk about the part of the verse that says, "shall not doubt in his heart." To doubt simply means to differ. It means we do not agree with the Word or its truth in the context of our particular situation. While we have not used the word "doubt" until this point, this should sound familiar from when we talked about rejection and abandonment. To be believing is to lack doubt. This means that when we hear and we choose to accept, we believe in our hearts, and when we hold on to that belief and don't abandon it, there is no doubt in our hearts.

This doesn't mean that thoughts and feelings of doubt might try to attach themselves to your life, but rather that your belief in your heart exists outside of those thoughts and feelings. Often, people think that the thoughts and doubts in their heads have disqualified the faith in their hearts. That's not the case at all. As long as you keep the Word as your anchor and the belief in your heart, you will be able to access the kind of faith Jesus was talking about in Mark 11:23-24.

What I love about these verses is the sheer power of our faith that Jesus talks about. He literally says that your faith has the potential to move a mountain. This, by the way, is not an exaggeration or a metaphor. Jesus tells us that you can have whatever you say. If you can simply believe in your heart and confess with your mouth, you can achieve and obtain every promise the Bible has to offer.

> IF YOU CAN SIMPLY BELIEVE IN YOUR HEART AND CONFESS WITH YOUR MOUTH, YOU CAN ACHIEVE AND OBTAIN EVERY PROMISE THE BIBLE HAS TO OFFER

With this in mind, I want to take a closer look at verse 24, where it says, "Therefore I say unto you, What things soever ye desire, when ye pray, believe that ye receive them, and ye shall have them." If you think back to the last chapter, you'll remember that we talked about the tense of hope and faith. We said hope is in the future, and faith is in the now because Hebrews 11:1 says, "Now faith is..." This verse in Mark 11:24 further confirms that idea because it tells us that whatever we desire, to believe we receive when we pray, and we will have it. Faith is believing we receive when we pray. Not believing we will receive, but believing that we receive right now. That the moment we release our faith, it goes to work on our behalf. We might not see its physical effects in the temporal right away (like the fig tree Jesus cursed), but it is working immediately in the eternal to accomplish what we believe it will.

I want to talk specifically about this process of believing you receive when you pray. This is what I like to call the prayer of faith, and it is the vehicle for releasing our formed beliefs. Once you have heard the Word and accepted it as truth, you have formed the belief in your heart, and faith has been activated. Your next step is to believe you receive when you pray.

But what exactly does that mean? To clarify, when you believe you receive when you pray, you are not expecting to see an instantaneous result the second that you say amen. What it means is that the moment you release your faith through the words of your mouth, you know that it is working on your behalf immediately to go into the eternal realm and pull your completed promise into the temporal. Like we talked about in the last chapter, it is not a matter of your faith creating the thing you are believing for, it is a matter of your faith obtaining it. When you believe you receive when you pray, you know that the promise you are believing for is yours the very moment you pray. You might not see it immediately, but you know it's on its way.

> WHEN YOU BELIEVE YOU RECEIVE WHEN YOU PRAY, YOU KNOW THAT THE PROMISE YOU ARE BELIEVING FOR IS YOURS THE VERY MOMENT YOU PRAY

One dangerous mistake I see a lot of people make is feeling like they have to repeat their prayer over and over again. If you'll think back to when we talked about hearing the Word, we determined that it only took hearing one time to produce faith. The same is true for releasing faith. You only have to believe you receive when you pray one time. Read that carefully. It's not that you have only to believe one time (your belief shouldn't change), it's that you have to believe you receive when you pray one time. This means when you pray and release your faith, you only do it once.

The overall goal is that you believe you receive when you pray the very first time. 1 John 5:14-15 (KJV) says:

> "And this is the confidence that we have in him, that, if we ask anything according to his will, he heareth us: And if we know that he hear us, whatsoever we ask, we know that we have the petitions that we desired of him."

I love these verses even more in the Message version, where it says:

> "And how bold and free we then become in his presence, freely asking according to his will, sure that he's listening. And if we're confident that he's listening, we know that what we've asked for is as good as ours."

This is why we only have to ask God one time. Because when we ask, He hears us. And when He hears, our promise is as good as ours. I often say it like this: any prayer you've prayed more than once has not had full belief in it. That might sound a little harsh, and I certainly don't mean for that to be deflating in your faith journey. If you've prayed a prayer more than once, don't worry! You're officially a part of the club with literally every other believer who has walked the face of the Earth. We've all been there, and we've all done it. But as we grow and learn more about the process of faith, the importance of believing we receive when we pray becomes completely clear.

OH YEAH? PROVE IT.

I'd like to take a few steps back before we take our next steps forward. Let's talk about the value of the Word of God when it comes to releasing your faith. If you'll remember our last chapter, we talked about our faith being the "title deed." It is our proof of ownership. What does that title deed give us ownership to? The promises of the Word of God. We know that grace has provided everything we could ever want or need and that faith obtains it, but as we've repeatedly discussed, faith requires hearing and hearing by the Word of God to be formed.

It is vital to recognize that the Bible is the key to unlocking every single thing that you desire. We'll talk more about this in the next chapter, but I cannot overstate the sheer dependency your faith has on God's Word. Everything you need can be traced to a scripture.

When I think about faith as being "evidence," I instantly picture a courtroom type setting. Us releasing our faith is almost like presenting a case to God. Not because God needs to be convinced of His power or ability, but rather because He needs us to be fully convinced of His power and ability to move on our behalf. If you think about it, that's really what faith is. Faith is not used to "move" God to do anything; He's already accomplished everything through grace. Faith is all about our belief in His ability to fulfill what He's already provided for us. So when I say we're "presenting our case" to God, we are really just presenting our case to prove that we are convinced.

> FAITH IS ALL ABOUT OUR BELIEF IN HIS ABILITY TO FULFILL WHAT HE'S ALREADY PROVIDED FOR US

With that in mind, have you ever seen or heard of a court case that only had one piece of evidence? I'm sure there are some cases out there that have, but my guess is that the success rate is very low. Why? Because evidence is based on an accumulation of knowledge. Lawyers and attorneys spend hours, weeks, and months gathering information that they can to prove their point because that is what is required to have a successful case. So if faith operates as the "evidence," and evidence is based on the accumulation of knowledge, don't you think it's important to gather as much information we can about what we're believing for? The Bible answers that question for us in 2 Corinthians 13:1 (AMP), where it says, "every fact shall be sustained and confirmed by the testimony of two or three witnesses." This means whenever you have a need or desire, you should accumulate as much knowledge as you can from the Word.

Your case needs to be airtight. Again, not to convince God, but so that you are completely convinced of all God can do in your situation. You do this by finding as many scriptures as you can to confirm your desire. And trust me, the Word contains every title to every promise you could ever believe for. As you find more evidence, you build your understanding and thus your trust in the reliability of the Word, which will help to activate your faith at even greater levels.

One of the best examples of this was a story I heard a while ago. A particular pastor did a lot of traveling and was looking for a plane. Obviously, he couldn't just go out and buy one because well, planes are expensive. So he began believing God for it. Some time went by, and he hosted a guest speaker (who had no previous knowledge of the pastor's need for an airplane). As the guest speaker was ministering, he turned to the pastor and said, "your plane is in Ecclesiastes 10:20." The pastor opened his Bible and read the verse, which says, "For a bird of the air may carry your voice, And a bird in flight may tell the matter."

Clearly, the Bible didn't say "you can have an airplane to fly in," but this verse gave validity to the desire of the pastor's heart. It's important to note the guest speaker didn't give the pastor the money to purchase a plane, he didn't tell him some crazy miracle was going to happen, and he didn't give him a detailed plan to purchase a plane. The guest speaker gave him a scripture.* Why? Because the Word of God gives us access to every promise we could ever want or need. If you're ever unsure of that truth, just remember that if God can give someone a scripture to receive an airplane, there is undoubtedly a scripture for your situation.

*P.S. that pastor ended up getting his airplane.

Now you might be wondering, "how do I find these promises in the Bible?" The good news is you don't have to be a Bible scholar or theologian to discover scriptures about your specific desire or need. Every time I preach about faith, I always encourage everyone to start by Googling what they want or need. For example, if you need restoration, just go to Google and type in "scriptures about restoration." If you want financial prosperity, type in "scriptures about financial prosperity." If you want healing, type in "scriptures about healing." Whatever it is that you need, start by Googling it. There will be more scriptures than you'll know what to do with.

From that foundation, you can begin to meditate in the accumulation of truth from the Word and form the beliefs in your heart. It doesn't have to be a challenging or complicated process. The tools are there for a reason, why not use them? Whatever it takes to find your scriptures, your proofs, your title deeds, do it. The sooner you hear, the sooner faith can be formed, and the sooner it can be released.

CHAPTER SIX
CONFESSION

I remember there was a time when my wife and I were faced with an uncertain situation. We didn't really know how to handle it, and we were both feeling extremely uneasy. I was at work, and though I didn't know how the situation was going to work out, I just remember saying over and over to myself, "whosoever shall believe with his heart and confess with his mouth shall have whatsoever he says." I must have quoted that scripture from Romans 10:9 at least a hundred times. Suddenly, after repeating that scripture over and over, I felt like I had risen to a place of faith in my heart, and I was ready to release it. I knew I had formed the belief enough in my heart to release it with my mouth. Once I had released my faith, the situation turned out fine and worked out with no issues whatsoever.

This is an example of the process of faith. See, I didn't just form the faith in my heart and leave it there. Once I felt like I had risen to the place of belief that God was going to move on my behalf, I released that faith. Here's the thing: until your heart and your mouth connect, you won't be able to release mountain-moving faith. As we just spent the entire last chapter learning, it is not enough to just have beliefs; we must also release them.

> UNTIL YOUR HEART AND YOUR MOUTH CONNECT, YOU WON'T HAVE MOUNTAIN-MOVING FAITH

The vehicle to release your faith is your words. Isaiah 51:16 (KJV) tells us,

> "And I have put my words in thy mouth, and I have covered thee in the shadow of mine hand, that I may plant the heavens, and lay the foundations of the earth, and say unto Zion, Thou art my people."

Here God tells us that He is planting the heavens and laying the foundations of the Earth with one thing: words. And not just any words; His words in our mouths. This is how you obtain the promises of God. You speak the words of God through the only place that you can find His words: the Bible.

If we look back to Mark 11:23 (KJV), we see Jesus tells us this:

> "For verily I say unto you, That whosoever shall say unto this mountain, Be thou removed, and be thou cast into the sea; and shall not doubt in his heart, but shall believe that those things which he saith shall come to pass; he shall have whatsoever he saith."

Question: does this scripture say that you can have whatever God says you can have? If you look closely, that's not the case. Jesus says that you can have whatever you say. This is extremely important to understand before we look closer at confession. One of the keys that Jesus highlighted in this verse is that you will never have what the Word says you can have until you start saying it. The promises of the Bible are not automatic; we don't just receive them by default or through osmosis. You don't have what God says you can have; you have whatever you say God says you can have. This means forming and releasing faith to obtain God's promises comes down to one major factor: you. The beliefs you form in your heart and the words you confess with your mouth determine the promises you obtain from God.

CONFESSION IS A LAW

No pressure or anything... Just kidding! There really is no pressure. You already know how to form beliefs, and we've already started to talk about how to release them. Once you understand the role of confession, you'll be fully equipped to operate in faith. So let's take a closer look at confession.

First, it's important to note that confession is a law. Matthew 12:33-37 (NKJV) says:

> "Either make the tree good and its fruit good, or else make the tree bad and its fruit bad; for a tree is known by its fruit. Brood of vipers! How can you, being evil, speak good things? For out of the abundance of the heart the mouth speaks. A good man out of the good treasure of his heart brings forth good things, and an evil man out of the evil treasure brings forth evil things. But I say to you that for every idle word men may speak, they will give account of it in the day of judgment. For by

your words you will be justified, and by your words you will be condemned."

As we can see in verse 37, we are justified by our words, and by our words, we are condemned. This is the law of confession: the words that we speak create the reality we live in, whether good or bad. Even if we don't realize confession is a law, or see it, we are still bound to the reality that it creates in our lives.

Perhaps one of the greatest illustrations of this is James 3:2-7 (MSG), where it says:

> "If you could find someone whose speech was perfectly true, you'd have a perfect person, in perfect control of life. A bit in the mouth of a horse controls the whole horse. A small rudder on a huge ship in the hands of a skilled captain sets a course in the face of the strongest winds. A word out of your mouth may seem of no account, but it can accomplish nearly anything—or destroy it! It only takes a spark, remember, to set off a forest fire. A careless or wrongly placed word out of your mouth can do that. By our speech we can ruin the world, turn harmony to chaos, throw mud on a reputation, send the whole world up in smoke and go up

in smoke with it, smoke right from the pit of hell. This is scary: You can tame a tiger, but you can't tame a tongue—it's never been done. The tongue runs wild, a wanton killer. With our tongues we bless God our Father; with the same tongues we curse the very men and women he made in his image. Curses and blessings out of the same mouth!"

Alright, well, after reading that, we can basically wrap up this chapter. I'm kidding, of course. In all seriousness, these verses perfectly sum up the power of our confession. I love where it says, "A word out of your mouth may seem of no account, but it can accomplish nearly anything—or destroy it!" This is what confession can do: anything. The author of James likens your words to a rudder of a ship or a bit in a horse's mouth. That simply means that your confession reveals the course of your life.

YOUR MOUTH DICTATES YOUR DIRECTION

Your mouth dictates your direction. And most importantly, your body is bound to the reality that your mouth creates.

Because your confession is so vital to the direction of your life, it is crucial to understand what your confession is directed by. As we read a while ago in Matthew 12:34, "for out of the abundance of the heart the mouth speaketh." The Message version says it even better: "It's your heart, not the dictionary, that gives meaning to your words." Your heart is what directs your mouth. Another way to say it is that the words you speak are an overflow of your heart.

Think about it this way. Have you ever been mad about something? Maybe someone did something that really bothered you. You spend the whole day thinking about how that person messed up and how angry you are with them. The next time you see them, do you think you'll be showering them with compliments and positive words? Probably not. In fact, it's just the opposite. You'll likely express your anger by saying something rude or unkind because that's what you've been thinking about all day. We've all been there. And all the married people said, "Amen."

All jokes aside, this is what happens with everything in life. Whatever we allow into our hearts determines the words that come out of our mouths. What's dangerous about this truth is, if we aren't careful about what we let in our hearts, then the wrong things can come out of our mouths. Think of your heart like soil. You can't plant an apple seed and then expect to have a banana tree. It doesn't work like that. What we plant in our hearts is what produces the harvest for our lives. Matthew 6:22-23 (AMP) says it best:

> "The eye is the lamp of the body; so if your eye is clear [spiritually perceptive], your whole body will be full of light [benefiting from God's precepts]. But if your eye is bad [spiritually blind], your whole body will be full of darkness [devoid of God's precepts]. So if the [very] light inside you [your inner self, your heart, your conscience] is darkness, how great and terrible is that darkness!

As we can see, it all starts with what we allow in our eyes and our ears. When we consume the wrong things, we plant the wrong seeds in our hearts. When we plant the wrong seeds, we speak the wrong words. When we speak the wrong words, we lead our bodies in the wrong direction.

> WHAT WE PLANT IN OUR HEARTS IS WHAT PRODUCES THE HARVEST FOR OUR LIVES

This is why we must allow our hearts to be saturated with the Word of God. And this is especially why the foundation of our faith and beliefs has to be the Word of God. Because if the Word isn't forming your beliefs and shaping your confession, then your flesh is. Just like we just read in Matthew 6:23, if there is darkness in your heart, how great and terrible is that darkness. The only seed that can produce a bountiful harvest in your life is the Word. Proverbs 23:7 (KJV) even tells us, "for as he thinketh in his heart, so is he." We must guard our hearts and defend against any untruths that try to plant themselves there.

If you base the beliefs in your heart on anything other than what the Bible says, whether it be your thoughts, feelings, perceptions, opinions (yours or someone else's), your past experiences, or even your own ability, you will not see the right harvest in your life. Notice I didn't say you wouldn't receive a harvest, I just said you wouldn't receive the right harvest. Remember, it's just as easy to receive the promises of God from our words as it is to receive destruction. James 3:6 (MSG) reminds us that "by our speech we can ruin the world, turn harmony to chaos, throw mud on a reputation, send the whole world up in smoke and go up in smoke with it." This is the law of confession: our words bring life, or they bring death; by them, we are justified, or we are condemned. This is why we can't allow our hearts and beliefs to be formed by our flesh: our soul (mind, will, and emotions) and our body. Because ultimately, what is planted in our hearts will come out of our mouths, thus activating the law of confession.

You might have read that and thought to yourself, "oh no, I'm in trouble!" Because maybe you've said things that have the capacity to cause damage or are based in the flesh. I want to take a moment and let you know that there is no need to be discouraged. We have all said things that can cause damage. And to be honest, I say things out of my flesh often. The beginning of James 3, which we read when we first started talking about confession, literally says, "If you could find someone whose speech was perfectly true, you'd have a perfect person, in perfect control of life." As far as I know, the only perfect person to walk the Earth was Jesus. The Bible is telling us that everyone makes mistakes with our words; it's human nature. Our goal is not to be perfect, but rather to try our best.

In Matthew 15:13 (AMP), Jesus is dealing with a situation with the Pharisees, and He says these words, "Every plant which My heavenly Father did not plant will be torn up by the roots." If you've spoken any negative words, it's okay. It's just a matter of uprooting those words and replacing them with the right ones. Good words uproot bad seeds; good words are like a shovel digging up the weeds in a garden. Don't think that you are disqualified because of words you have spoken in the past, dig them up with the best words we have: the truths of the Word of God. And then plant those truths in place of the bad seeds.

> GOOD WORDS UPROOT BAD SEEDS; GOOD WORDS ARE LIKE A SHOVEL DIGGING UP THE WEEDS IN A GARDEN

Moving forward, we must always be sure to keep our hearts and beliefs fastened to the truth of the Word. When we do, we can be confident that we will produce the promises of the Word. Matthew 12:35 (KJV) reminds us that "a good man out of the good treasure of his heart brings forth good things…" I love how this verse uses the phrase "good treasure." It reminds me of how James 3 tells us that the mouth is the rudder for the direction of our lives. Not to get all Pirates of the Caribbean on you, but these verses together kind of make this sound like a treasure hunt, especially in the context of faith. The Word is like our map; it shows us where to go and what we'll find. Our words are what we use to steer the ship to get there. As long as you keep your heart connected to the "good treasure" of the Word, you keep your mouth speaking good things. And ultimately, you'll see the treasure of those good things come to pass when the promise is fulfilled.

One final thing to note is that confession is not what creates your promises. While confession might create your reality, it is not what is materializing the promises you are believing for. Remember, grace has already created everything that we could ever need or want in life, and faith is simply obtaining those wants and needs. Confession is just agreeing with what's already been created in order for faith to pull it into the temporal from the eternal. Our words don't create anything; they just agree with what grace has already provided and what faith can obtain.

HOW CONFESSION WORKS

Now that we understand the law of confession and how powerful it is, it's important to understand how it fits into the process of faith. Confession has two main roles when it comes to faith: creating your reality and strengthening your beliefs. The first role, creating your reality, has to do with using confession to release faith. Whereas the other role, strengthening your beliefs, has to do with using confession after you've released faith. We'll look at the other role of confession in the next chapter, but for now, let's look specifically at using confession to release faith.

When we talked about using the prayer of faith to release the beliefs we had activated in our hearts, we talked about believing you receive when you pray. To recap, Mark 11:23-24 tell us:

> "For verily I say unto you, That whosoever shall say unto this mountain, Be thou removed, and be thou cast into the sea; and shall not doubt in his heart, but shall believe that those things which he saith shall come to pass; he shall have whatsoever he saith. Therefore I say unto you, What things soever ye desire, when ye

pray, believe that ye receive them, and ye shall have them."

One of the most important things about this scripture, and I hit on this at the beginning of this chapter, is that Jesus says, "whosoever say unto this mountain" and "he shall have whatsoever he saith." Again, this reveals the power of confession.

But how does this work when it comes to faith? The very first place we use confession in the process of faith is in the "believe we receive when we pray." Imagine this: I have a very serious question for my wife; something beyond important, such as where she wants to go to dinner. I call her on the phone, and she answers, but I say nothing at all. In my mind and heart, I'm asking her my question: "where do you want to go for dinner?" But in reality, all she hears is silence. What is the key to my wife answering my question? My words. Even if we were in the same room and she was looking at me, if I'm not communicating the question, she wouldn't be able to give me an answer.

It works the same way with God. Why would we expect God to give us an answer if we never ask Him the question? James 4:2 (NLT) even tells us, "Yet you don't have what you want because you don't ask God for it." While God knows our desires and our needs, it is our action that produces His response. Matthew 7:7 (KJV) says, "Ask, and it shall be given you," it doesn't say "think about it, and God will give it to you" or even "believe it, and God will give it to you." When you pray, you are having a conversation with God. You are putting words to the inner workings of your heart. So when you believe you receive when you pray, you are utilizing confession to release the beliefs you have formed in your heart.

> WHILE GOD KNOWS OUR DESIRES AND OUR NEEDS, IT IS OUR ACTION THAT PRODUCES HIS RESPONSE

When it comes down to it, confession doesn't just "fit into" the release side of faith; it *is* the release side of faith. The key to releasing your faith properly is using the right words. Or a better way to say it is the key to releasing your faith is using the Word. The only "right words" to use when you pray are the ones that you used to form your faith: the ones from the Word. Whatever scriptures you used to form your faith, you also use to release your faith. Your confession should simply be the verbal emphasis of your title deed to the promise you're believing for. You don't have to have some eloquent and beautifully crafted prayer to get God's attention. You simply need His Word and your request, all backed by your belief.

With that being said, I want to give you a template, if you will, for when you "believe you receive when you pray." As a big disclaimer, this is not the only way to release your faith. It's not even "the right way" because I don't think there's one right way to do this. I just want to give you an idea of how you can release your faith so that you recognize it's not some mystic and big thing. You can put your own spin on it, and how you approach God is your own business. But here's an idea of what releasing your faith looks like:

> "Dear Heavenly Father, I come to you now in the name of Jesus and thank you for who you are. I come to you today, and I need (or want) INSERT YOUR NEED OR WANT HERE. According to your Word in INSERT YOUR SCRIPTURE REFERENCE(S) HERE, you say, "INSERT SCRIPTURE(S) HERE." Father, you say that when I believe I receive when I pray, I can

have it. I believe in my heart that you will meet YOUR NEED OR WANT, and I receive it now as I confess it with my mouth. I thank you, Father, that I will see my promise come to pass through the power of my faith and the abundance of your grace. In Jesus' name, I pray, Amen."

That's it. In the 20 seconds that it took you to pray that prayer, you have just released your faith. As long as you believe the Word in your heart and that you receive it, and then confess it with your mouth, you have released your faith. And it is released faith and released faith only that can obtain the promises of God.

PUTTING IT ALL TOGETHER

Before we move on, let's consider releasing faith in a practical sense by looking at an example. Your friend Sally is sick. She has been to every doctor in town and has finally received a diagnosis that she has a rare skin disease. It's not life-threatening, but it's causing her a lot of pain, and she wants to be healed. As we've discussed in-depth, Jesus has made way for every desire of our heart through His death on the cross and our salvation. That sacrifice has already made way for Sally to be healed. Now, she simply has to find truths in God's Word and accept them to form the belief in her heart.

She goes to Google and searches "scriptures about healing" and finds 1 Peter 2:24 (KJV) that says, "Who his own self bare our sins in his own body on the tree, that we, being dead to sins, should live unto righteousness: by whose stripes ye were healed." Sally reads this scripture, and she agrees. She knows with all of her heart that Jesus can heal her body. Sally's next step is to believe she receives when she prays. This part is so extremely important. Sally knows there is no doubt in her heart and so she bows her head and prays, using her confession to release the faith she's formed in her heart. She says something similar to the template I shared a few pages ago: "Dear Heavenly Father, I come to you today in need of healing. I know that according to your Word in Mark 11:24 that if I believe I receive when I pray that I will have whatever I desire. 1 Peter 2:24 tells me that by your stripes, I am healed, and I believe that with all my heart. So right now, I thank you, Father, for my healing. I believe in my heart, and I confess with my mouth that you are working complete and total healing in my body."

This example, though extremely simplified and completely hypothetical, perfectly illustrates the process of forming and releasing faith. Sally has a desire, finds a promise in the Word that confirms her desire, accepts it, believes in her heart that she receives it, and prays and confesses it in her life. So what comes next? You might think Sally's job is done once she's released faith, but actually, it's just begun.

CHAPTER SEVEN
NOW WHAT?

Hey, you've made it to the last chapter! You've learned everything you need to know about forming and releasing faith. As a recap... You know faith is what you believe and that it comes by hearing and hearing by the Word of God. You know faith is formed in the heart when you hear it and accept it, and that you should watch out for rejecting and abandoning the truth of the Word. You also know faith is the substance of things hoped for and the evidence of things unseen and that it simply obtains what grace has provided in the eternal and brings it into the temporal. You know forming faith is important but means nothing if you don't release it. And you know the only way to release it is through your words when you believe you receive when you pray. I'd like to congratulate you because now you are a faith expert! If you didn't know, you actually get a prize for being a faith expert: it's called waiting.

Sorry if you thought it would be something a little more glamorous, but in reality, this is typically the prize of our faith: Time. Unless it is a miraculous encounter, which is not impossible, the time between releasing faith and seeing a promise come to pass is definitely more than overnight. If it took time for the fig tree that Jesus cursed to show signs of the faith that He used, then it's highly likely that we'll have a waiting period for our promise too. I don't say that to discourage you from using faith, because this shouldn't be the case at all. It's just important to recognize that though the exchange of faith is instant, we might not see its effects immediately. That doesn't mean faith isn't working, and it doesn't mean that you should stop believing. In fact, once you've formed and released your beliefs, your faith journey is just beginning.

And don't let that overwhelm you. You are fully equipped to handle the time between releasing your faith and receiving your promise because this book has given you everything you need to know. How is that possible if this entire book has been about forming and releasing faith? It's simple. The principles used to form and release faith are the same principles used to sustain and strengthen faith.

> THE PRINCIPLES USED TO FORM AND RELEASE FAITH ARE THE SAME PRINCIPLES USED TO SUSTAIN AND STRENGTHEN FAITH

BACK TO THE BEGINNING

Just as much as it takes the same principles, it takes the same promises. Forming and releasing faith is the easiest part, whereas the maintenance of your faith is often the most challenging. The most dangerous thing to do when you're in faith is to abandon your beliefs. Remember how we read in Mark 4:17-19 how we learned about affliction and persecution that arises for the Word's sake? And not only affliction and persecution, but also the cares of the world, the deceitfulness of riches, and the lusts of other things.

This reveals that not only do you have to withstand time while you wait for your promise, you also have to withstand all of the trials, tests, and troubles that are arising specifically for your promise. Once you release your belief, the enemy is on assignment to get you to abandon it. I don't want to dance around this, because I don't want to give you a false impression of this process. There will be a lot of moments that you feel like you can't believe anymore — situations, circumstances, negative people, opportunities for offense, etc. You'll likely see all or at least a few of these things coming for your faith. But you must choose not to abandon. Don't let go of your faith, and don't abandon the investments that you've made. There are quite a few keys we're about to cover that sustain your faith and strengthen it.

Before we get there, I briefly want to acknowledge something. Because you might be wondering, "what if I do abandon my beliefs?" I know I've definitely abandoned my beliefs before, and honestly, I think everyone has at some point. Sometimes it is incredibly challenging to hold on to faith when everything is trying to take it from you.

The good news is that even if you do abandon faith, you are not disqualified. You have an unlimited supply of chances to start the process of faith again. You simply have to hear again to start over. It's like a reset button; go back to the beginning and start the process over from page one of this book. You'll never be disqualified from using faith, but I will note that starting the process over does invalidate the time that you have put into believing. Ultimately the abandonment of your beliefs is an abandonment of the investment of time that you have placed in your beliefs. But, you are never denied any opportunity to start over again.

HOPE

While you have every opportunity to start the process of faith over again if you abandon your beliefs, we want to avoid abandoning at all costs. Not because it invalidates our future faith, but because it voids our past investment. We should view our faith in a promise as an investment; it becomes more valuable over time. The more time that you have in it, the more valuable it becomes, and the less you'll want to let go of it. While time increases the value of the investment, there are other factors that can contribute to the value. There are three main keys that can help maximize your investment of faith.

> WE SHOULD VIEW OUR FAITH IN A PROMISE AS AN INVESTMENT; IT BECOMES MORE VALUABLE OVER TIME

The first key to maximizing your faith is hope. If you think back to when we talked about the difference between hope and faith, we said that hope is confident expectation with joyful anticipation. We clarified that faith and hope have different functions, and that hope in the Word activates faith. Another extremely important function of hope comes in after faith has been released. Hebrews 6:19 (TPT) reveals that "We have this certain hope like a strong, unbreakable anchor holding our souls to God himself." After faith has been released, hope becomes our anchor to the truth of the Word. It is what keeps us fastened to the promises that we are believing for. Hope might be a poor receiver, but it's a great waiter.

AFTER FAITH HAS BEEN RELEASED, HOPE BECOMES OUR ANCHOR TO THE TRUTH OF THE WORD

In the process of forming and releasing faith, hope is pivotal in providing the expectation of the promise to be received. Once we have a revelation of the truth of the Word, it becomes our confident expectation; this then opens the door to forming our faith. But I think that hope's greatest function is after faith has been released.

When we first talked about hearing the Word to activate faith, I told you that you don't have to hear more than once to believe. This is still true. But, hearing the promise you used to form your faith is what will allow you to sustain and strengthen it. The hope that activated your faith when you heard it is what you return to after you released it. That's why I love how the Bible refers to hope as an anchor for your soul. I always envisioned it like a rope tied around your waist that was connected to the Bible. The Bible was closed, but the rope was still there, keeping you tethered to its truth.

If you find yourself struggling to hold on to faith once you've released it, return to its root. Go back and read your promises. When you stay connected to the truth of the Word, you're anchoring yourself so that you can receive the promises you're believing for.

CONFESSION

The next key to maximizing your investment of faith is your confession. One of my favorite stories about faith is from the Father of Faith himself, Dr. Kenneth Hagin. I'll never forget hearing him tell a story about a time when he was ministering, and he ended up praying for people. God was doing great miracles and moving mightily; people were being healed instantaneously and seeing instant miracles. He got to a little boy who had clubbed feet; he was standing with his mother right behind him. He prayed over the little boy, and he said that he felt more power go into the boy than anyone he prayed for, even the ones who experienced great and instantaneous miracles. What was crazy was that the boy's clubbed feet were not instantly healed. Even though Brother Hagin felt more power going into the little boy than any other person that night, the results were not immediately visible. Brother Hagin turned to the mother and said something I will never forget. He said, "Keep the switch of faith turned on. Every time you think of it, say and thank God the healing power is working a healing and a cure."

This story always brings me back to the importance of confession. Brother Hagin said to keep the switch of faith turned on. Meaning, whenever the mother thought of her son's feet, she was to speak of his healing. This is the exact way we are to use confession after releasing our beliefs. Remember, when we first use confession, we are using it to release our beliefs. Once we've done that, confession takes on a new role. Confession after faith has been released is simply strengthening your beliefs.

> CONFESSION AFTER FAITH HAS BEEN RELEASED IS SIMPLY STRENGTHENING YOUR BELIEFS

The benefit of confession is identical to hope after releasing faith; it keeps you connected to the promises. Remember, if the heart and mouth don't connect, you won't have mountain-moving faith. Out of the abundance of the heart, the mouth speaks. So whatever is coming out of your mouth is simply a reflection of your heart and what you believe. This is why it is just as important to speak the Word after you have released faith as it is when you release faith.

It's important to note how to confess the Word because even though it is of equal importance, it does not have the same function. Confession, when you believe you receive when you pray, is all about releasing faith; confession after you do so, is to strengthen your faith. As we learned, confession doesn't actually create anything; it is simply an agreement with what has already been created. Once you've released faith, confession is all about connecting yourself back to God's promises to avoid being connected to the circumstances that stand in front of you.

Confession after releasing faith is based in thanksgiving. I believe the key factor in this is hope. When you continually return to the truth of the promises that you are believing for, you are anchored in the confident expectation of receiving them. The second half of hope is joyful anticipation; as you wait for the promises that faith is obtaining for you, it is important to look forward, not with dread, but with joy. That confident expectation with joyful anticipation should overflow into thanksgiving. Colossians 2:7 (AMP) says it like this:

> "having been deeply rooted [in Him] and now being continually built up in Him and [becoming increasingly more] established in your faith, just as you were taught, and overflowing in it with gratitude."

This verse reveals that the overflow of our established faith should be our gratitude and our thanksgiving. Philippians 4:6 (AMP) says it best,

> "Do not be anxious or worried about anything, but in everything [every circumstance and

situation] by prayer and petition with thanksgiving, continue to make your [specific] requests known to God."

It is through thanksgiving that we continue to make our requests known to God. We don't need to ask again, because we know that we believe we receive when we pray, but we can thank God for the promises that our faith is obtaining. Just like Brother Hagin told the young boy's mother, "Every time you think of it, say and thank God the healing power is working a healing and a cure," we should thank God for the specific promise we are believing for.

For example, let's think back to Sally, who had a skin disease. After releasing her faith, Sally would want to spend time revisiting her scripture that she found in 1 Peter 2:24. As she re-reads her scriptures, she is anchoring herself in the hope of the Word. Then, Sally would want to keep her confession up by saying, "Thank you, Father, that by your stripes, I am healed. Thank you for working a healing and a cure in my body." Just like Brother Hagin said, every time that you think about it: say. Confession is necessary because it keeps our mouth anchored to the truth of the Word and keeps us on track to receive the promises that faith is obtaining.

It is important to always keep your confession on the truth of the Word and not the situation, circumstances, or troubles in front of you. As a general rule, if the Bible doesn't say it, neither should you. Keeping your confession grounded in the promise and not influenced by the circumstances is one of the most important keys to maintaining and strengthening your faith once it has been released.

BY FAITH, NOT SIGHT

The third key to maximizing your investment of faith is to walk by faith and not by sight. I love how 2 Corinthians 5:7 in The Passion Translation tells us, "for we live by faith, not by what we see with our eyes." Like we covered at the beginning of this chapter, the waiting period between releasing faith and receiving the promise is the most challenging part. Whether it's time or trials or tests, there are so many things coming against our faith trying to get us to abandon it. 1 Peter 4:12 (AMP) even tells us,

> "Beloved, do not be surprised at the fiery ordeal which is taking place to test you [that is, to test the quality of your faith], as though

something strange or unusual were happening to you."

And we get even more good news in 1 Peter 1:7 (AMP), where it says,

"so that the genuineness of your faith, which is much more precious than gold which is perishable, even though tested and purified by fire, may be found to result in [your] praise and glory and honor at the revelation of Jesus Christ."

Basically, no one is exempt from the trials that come for faith. In fact, those trials and circumstances are what enable faith to be brought to maturity. When challenges or troubles arrive, don't think you're alone or doing something wrong. It's just the opposite: trials and troubles for the sake of your faith are a signal that you're doing the right thing.

> TRIALS AND TROUBLES FOR THE SAKE OF YOUR FAITH ARE A SIGNAL THAT YOU'RE DOING THE RIGHT THING

It is in these moments where we must rely on our hope and our confession to carry us through the trials and troubles. We have to continually dwell in the truth of the Word and speak it. That is what it means to walk by faith and not by sight — standing up to the challenges that we face, not with our own ability or own strength, but with the power of the Word of God. Do not be discouraged or dismayed at the sight of trouble; simply choose to walk by faith and not by what you see.

GROWING FAITH

A huge misconception I see a lot of people make about faith is that it grows. Specifically, when people think they have to have a certain amount of faith to be able to believe for certain things. Some people might think that to believe for "big things" they have to have "big faith." I've never agreed with the idea that your faith has a "strength" to it. Faith comes by hearing and hearing by the Word, not by our own strength. If faith's ability were based on how much we had, it would be human-based and an unfair playing field. This would mean if I have "more faith" than you do, I could achieve and obtain more things than you can. The Bible says God is not a respecter of persons, or as the Message version in Acts 10:34 says, "It's God's own truth, nothing could be plainer: God plays no favorites!" God doesn't play favorites and ultimately, faith doesn't grow in terms of its ability to produce a promise.

Remember how we talked about the Roman centurion and how he had "great faith"? Don't forget he was a one-time hearer. Beyond God not being a respecter of persons, I never understood the concept of "growing faith" because the Bible has so many stories that show people receiving their promise after hearing one time. Even Jesus Himself says in Matthew 17:20 (NIV), "if you have faith as small as a mustard seed, you can say to this mountain, 'Move from here to there,' and it will move. Nothing will be impossible for you.'"

Faith is an obtainer, not a container. It is not "how much" we have or use, but rather how we use it. I don't believe that your faith grows in terms of its ability to produce promises, but 2 Thessalonians 1:3 (KJV) says "We are bound to thank God always for you, brethren, as it is meet, because that your faith groweth exceedingly, and the charity of every one of you all toward each other aboundeth;" Here we see that faith does in fact grow. But if faith doesn't grow in terms of its ability to receive promises, how does it grow? I believe faith grows after we release it. Meaning, our faith is strengthened after it is released.

Specifically, I think it is our capacity to believe that grows. Believing and confessing are the first steps in faith. Arguably, that is when our faith is at its most infant stage. You don't have a full concept of what you're believing; you're just believing. Over time, as you dwell in the hope and confess it, you increase your capacity to believe; you are strengthening your faith. Hebrews 11:11 (TPT) says this:

> "Sarah's faith embraced the miracle power to conceive even though she was barren and was past the age of childbearing, for the authority of her faith[a] rested in the One who made the promise, and she tapped into his faithfulness."

This particular scripture is referring to Sarah when she and Abraham were believing for a son. They were far past the age to conceive a child, yet they still believed. The external circumstance seemed far greater than what they were able to handle, yet they still believed. This scripture reveals how. I love how it says the authority of her faith was found in the One who made the promise. Sarah tapped into God's faithfulness to see her promise come to pass. This is where her faith grew; she didn't know how God was going to do it, but she knew He would do it, and that was all that mattered. Think about it this way: a seed doesn't grow until after it's sown. The same is true with faith. Once we believe we receive when we pray, we have planted a seed of faith. As we wait for the harvest, we return to God's faithfulness, continually learning more about His character and His principles. Through a consistent returning to His Word, we are strengthening the beliefs we created from it, and ultimately, we are growing.

The greatest thing of all is that we are not just growing in faith for the current promise we are believing for but also the ones that we will believe for in the future. As we believe for more and see those promises come to pass, we are creating a foundation for future steps of faith. In this way, we are expanding our capacity to believe in the future. It is not because we have stronger faith, but because we have a greater

> EVERY PROMISE YOU RECEIVE IS A CATALYST FOR A FUTURE BELIEF BECAUSE IT KEEPS YOU ANCHORED TO THE TRUTH OF THE WORD ON A PERSONAL LEVEL

understanding of God's faithfulness. Every promise you receive is a catalyst for a future belief because it keeps you anchored to the truth of the Word on a personal level. As you believe for more, you'll see more.

WHEN IT'S ALL SAID AND DONE

No matter what you're believing for, faith is there to obtain every promise you could ever imagine. The process starts with what you believe and ends with how long you believe. Faith's expiration date is when you see your promise come to pass. Romans 8:24 (TPT) says this:

> "For this is the hope of our salvation. But hope means that we must trust and wait for what is still unseen. For why would we need to hope for something we already have?"

Just like it says, we don't need to use faith once the promise shows up. How silly would it be to believe for something that you already physically have? Once you receive your promise, your faith has fulfilled its mission. What does that mean for you? Until you see your promise come to pass, stay in faith because faith is still working. Often people say that seeing is believing, but with faith, it's just the opposite. With faith, we believe until we see.

No matter what desires or needs that you have, faith is here to help you fulfill them. Once you start the process of faith, hold on for dear life, with everything within you. 2 Corinthians 1:20 (TPT) tells us, "For all of God's promises find their "yes" of fulfillment in him. And as his "yes" and our "amen" ascend to God, we bring him glory!" Don't lose sight of your promises and always cling to the truth that enables you to receive them. Faith is your obtainer. Using it correctly will enable you to see every need and desire that you have fulfilled.

I pray this book has helped you develop a greater understanding of the nature and process of faith and that you can achieve everything you seek in life. I believe that with faith, you will obtain all the promises that await you in the Word of God and you will live your most empowered life.

ABOUT THE AUTHOR

Dr. Chris Sarno is an author, speaker, and pastor who wholeheartedly believes in the life changing power of God. Radically saved and filled with the Holy Spirit at age 24, Chris stepped into a new life in Christ and has never looked back. His desire to learn and grow in his faith led him to attend and graduate from Rhema Bible Training Center in Tulsa, Oklahoma.

With his passion bold and his purpose clear, Chris pursued what God had for him. Ultimately leading him and his wife, Liz, to plant what is now Relevant Church in Daytona Beach in 2004. In addition to pastoring, Chris travels the world as an evangelist, spreading the gospel message wherever he goes.

Chris and Liz are also the founders of the International Bible Training Center, a fully accredited, worldwide, online Bible College. They reside in Florida with their three wonderful children (Lauren, Luca, and Giana). To learn more about Chris and his ministry, visit www.chrissarno.tv.

LET US KNOW WHAT YOU'RE GETTING FROM THE BOOK

USE THE HASHTAG
#OBTAINABLEBOOK

CONNECT WITH PASTOR CHRIS SARNO
LEARN MORE AT CHRISSARNO.TV

CALL IT NOT AS TH IT WERE

Psalms 100:5

> Rejoice In The Lord ALWAYS
> Phil 4:4

Famous for His faithfulness

I'm Greatful because God is faithful

THANK GOD...
I GET TO GO THERE
PRAISE } w/ PRAYER + THANKSGIVING